BLOOD WAR

The Blood Covenant and Spiritual Warfare

by
Randy Hix

Legacy Ministries International, Inc.
Costa Mesa, California
In Cooperation with
EMBASSY PUBLISHING
Laguna Hills, California

Unless otherwise indicated, all Scripture quotations are taken from the King James Bible

Printed in the United States of America. All rights reserved under International Copyright Law. Contents and/or cover may not be reproduced in whole or in part in any form without expressed written consent of Legacy Ministries International, Inc

Blood War - The Blood Covenant and Spiritual Warfare
ISBN 1-879993-20-1
Copyright (c) 1994 by
Randall Hix / Legacy Ministries International, Inc.
P.O. Box 5370-565
Santa Ana, CA 92704

Published by Embassy Publishing
P. O. Box 3500
Laguna Hills, CA 92654

Cover design by:
Scott Hix Creative Designs
Legacy Ministries International
P.O. Box 5370-565
Santa Ana, CA 92704

For Speaking Engagements contact:
Randy Hix - Legacy Ministries International, Inc.
P.O. Box 5370-565
Santa Ana, CA 92704

Table of Contents

Introduction 1

WHAT IS SPIRITUAL WARFARE? 5

ARE YOU AN OVERCOMER 9

TO GOD BE THE GLORY 15
    Lost Relationship 17

WHAT IS A COVENANT? 21
    Contractual Living 22
    What is Integrity 24
    What is Marriage 25

TWO TYPES OF COVENANTS 31
    Unilateral Covenants 31
    Bilateral Covenants 31
    Where It All Began 32

WHERE POWER COMES FROM 35
    Natural Law and Spiritual Law 37
    The Law of Agreement 38

STRATEGY FOR VICTORY 43
    God's Covenant Crisis 46
    God's Strategy and Abram 48

GOD OF ABRAHAM, ISAAC & JACOB 53
    Why Circumcision 53
    Abraham's Blessing 55
    Three Patriarchs 58

THE RENEWED COVENANT 61
    Renewed Relationship 64

VICTORY THROUGH RELATIONSHIP 67
    The Lion, the Bear, and the Giant 69
    Right Attitude 69

THE NEW DEAL 75

THE SERPENT CRUSHER 79
    The "Seed' Revealed 79
    The Virgin Birth 81
    Finding a Representative 83
    If The Son Had Failed 84
    One Representative, Two Families 86
    Two Sacrifices 89
    The Covenant Lamb................. 90
    Blessing and Cursing 92
    Executor of a New Estate 93

A BETTER DEAL 97
    The Mystery of God 98
    New Mediator 100
    Better Promises 102

GET IN AND STAY IN 107
    Confession and Repentance.......... 110
    Divine Integrity 117

RELATIONAL AUTHORITY 121
    Unity and Authority 123
    Cooperative Fellowship 125
    Hearken to the Voice of the Lord. 127
    Follow His Commandments 128
    Do His Word 128

BE A WINNER 131
    Position Yourself 131
    Fear Not!.......................... 133
    FINAL NOTE 133

Dedication

This book is dedicated to the memory of Charles R. Hix, my father and to Ruby Hix, my Mom. Thanks for teaching me about Jesus and His love.

Special thanks to my wonderful wife Renee, for the motivation and encouragement I needed. To Sue Thompson, thanks "sis" for all your help with editing and proof reading. Also thank you Richard Fisher and Jayme Horton (soon to be Hix) for all the editing help.

Introduction

This book is not just for the exposing of a new truth. The truth of the Word of God can never be somebody's "New Revelation." Indeed the truth held within it's pages is eternal and no man can add to or take away from it. However, in generations past we have experienced God's divine plan to restore truth progressively to each generation. Since Martin Luther, and the Reformation credited to his teaching, we have seen a systematic revival of the truth of God's Word. We stand now on the threshold of the twenty first century. This century has seen an almost constant series of waves of revival, beginning with the restoration of Pentecost in Topeka, Kansas and Azusa Street in Los Angeles in 1906. The great revivalists of the early 1900's gave way to the evangelists of the thirties and forties. These in turn gave way to the healing revivals of the forties and fifties, which in turn made way for the pastors of the sixties, then the Jesus Movement and subsequent Charismatic Renewal of the seventies. Hand in hand with the Charismatic Renewal, was the restoration of the Teachers of the seventies and eighties.

Each generation has experienced it's own "movement." Each generation has seen the previous "movement" come against them and try to resist the message that their generation was to bring forth. From the Azusa Street revival until the present we have seen numerous restoration "moves," each with an element of Biblical truth to be placed as a building block onto previously restored truth.

Each generation has also had it's share of zealots who would take an element of Biblical truth and use it as a "battle-axe" against those who held to the more "traditional" way. The truth of every generation has survived in spite of those who, for whatever reasons, took that truth and tried to build something without the previous foundations undergirding it. It has rarely been the person with the original "revelation" that has misused it. Usually some of those individuals who were inspired by the "new truth" will set out to build their own empire, and as a result, will bring a reproach upon all those who simply desired to add to their foundations a fresh, divine, building block.

God is still adding building blocks of "revealed truth" today. Yet still today, we see the previous generation, who had their day of reformation truth and subsequent disdain, resisting and coming against all of those who are adding truth to their divine repertoire of revelation. Dr. Edwin Louis Cole has stated that, "Any truth taken to the exclusion of all other truth becomes error". I believe this statement would apply to those who take a "new revelation" to the exclusion of established truth; as well as those who take their "established" truth to the exclusion of any "new revelation." Between these two extremes walks the "Master Builder", Jesus Christ, the Author and Finisher (Builder) of our faith.

This brings me to the reason why the writing of this book is necessary and why the Lord Himself has called me to write it. It is not that I feel that no one has adequately covered the subject; they have. Nor is it because I feel that I alone have this revelation; I don't. It is my desire to build a bridge, from an "established" truth to a "new revealed truth".

The nineteen seventies and eighties saw the restoration of the faith teaching, or what we may now call the " Word of Faith" movement. Despite the fact that some are still grappling with this teaching, or even rejecting those who have taught or espoused it, we can safely say that it has become an established truth . While some took their liberties with this truth and distorted it for selfish means, its principles are firmly based in God's Word. I will not attempt to reteach that subject except where it applies.

As a result of the building block of the faith teaching, there has been a restoration of the ministry of the prophet, and a stronger manifestation of the gift of prophesy. This is due, in part, to the fact that we prophesy to the proportion of our faith.[a] It is also partly due to the intense times in which we live. Radical and intense times call for radical and intense people. The boldness of the faith message, combined with the ardent stance of the prophetic, has opened the way for a new "move" known as "Spiritual Warfare".

Some in the "Faith Camp" are opposed to what has been interpreted as spiritual warfare. Into this "riff" I would like to inject a book called "Blood War." A firm understanding of Covenant and how it relates to the blood of Jesus is the basis of faith. A firm understanding of faith is the very basis of successful

---

[a].Romans 12:6

"warfare"; "This is the victory that has overcome the world, even our faith".[a] The foundation of our victorious life in Jesus is the blood he shed on Calvary. The Apostle Paul tells us that we are still wrestling with principalities and powers, against the rulers of the darkness of this world, and against spiritual wickedness[b]. If our warfare is not carnal, or natural, and we do not wrestle with flesh and blood; our warfare must, by definition, be spiritual. The success of our spiritual warfare will be the result of our effectively using our spiritual weapons. "They overcame him by the blood of the Lamb and the word of their testimony, and loved not their lives unto death."[c]

These three parts of our weaponry combine the truth of the Blood Covenant (The blood of the Lamb), Faith (the word of their testimony), Radical intensity (Love not their lives unto death) and Spiritual Warfare (they overcame him). The bridge has been built. I pray this book will reveal it to you. Together we shall win this Blood War.

---

[a]. 1 John 5:4
[b]. Ephesians 6:12
[c]. Revelation 12:11

1
WHAT IS SPIRITUAL WARFARE?

For the past few years there has been a lot of communication about the message and ministry of "Spiritual Warfare". Many have come to accept it as a religious term that designates a branch of the Charismatic Church; or a phrase that speaks of a group of people that pray loud or preach hard. These misconceptions of the meaning of Spiritual Warfare have caused some to simply write it off as an extreme doctrine; or have caused others to overindulge their desire to be demonstrative by joining the commotion without understanding its meaning. Between these two extremes lies the truth concerning the realities of Spiritual Warfare.

The history of the Christian Church, in every age, is one of conflict. Each and every generation has faced opposition to the message of Christ to some degree. That conflict may have been in the form of public executions of those who espoused faith in Jesus Christ, or simply the pressure of a promiscuous society to conform to ungodly principles. Each new decade has seen a form of resistance and has called for a degree of aggression in order to fulfil the great commission to preach the gospel to every creature. What ever the conflict or time period in history, the source of any opposition to the gospel, can be linked to the source of all evil, Satan himself. Satan is not of this world, even though his aggression is focused on this world; and specifically, on those who would be followers of Jesus. His origin is in the spirit world and his aggression is first, and foremost, a spiritual aggression. Satan, the thief, comes only to kill, steal, and destroy, (John 10:10) therefore, pathway of the disciple of Jesus Christ is one of certain warfare.

Spiritual warfare has been a part of the ministry of the New Testament Church since it's birth on the Day of Pentecost. The Church in various cities, states, and countries has been facing opposition from spiritual forces all along. So why is the emphasis on "Spiritual Warfare" so prevalent in the Church today?

Jesus said that in the last days the condition of the world would be as it was in the days of Noah. Sin, sickness, and Satan, had so corrupted the earth that God found no other solution; but to destroy it in the flood. He found only one righteous man, Noah, to save the race of mankind while destroying the effects of sin on the earth. Today we can see the corruption of sin in the land again. We believe that these are indeed the last days as we see the condition of this world deteriorate as in the days of Noah. However, God has promised not to destroy the earth in another flood. Yet, sin, sickness, and Satan are raging. What can be done?

Because of the world's condition there needs to be a strong opposing force against sin. That force is the Church of Jesus Christ. The weapons of our "Warfare" are not of this world but mighty through God in order to pull down strongholds. (2 Corinthians 10:4) We are told in Ephesians six to put on the armor of God. Armor is used in warfare. The Apostle Paul states that we wrestle not against flesh and blood. However, we wrestle none the less.

The prophet Isaiah prophetically declared that no weapon formed against us shall prosper (Isaiah 54:17). Weapons are formed for "warfare." We are told to fight the good fight. We are instructed to endure hardship as good soldiers.

As the intensity of the days in which we live builds to a crescendo of sin and despair, we the church must accept the call to be a part of the Army of the Lord. We are assigned the task of bringing the Good News to a world in despair. It is a mission that is constantly plagued by conflict and opposition. It is a war for the souls of men and women, whether young or old. It is our place to be more than conquerors through Christ Jesus and the power of the Holy Spirit. It is indeed a "Spiritual Warfare". Jesus, the Captain of our Salvation is directing His Church into conflict and into victory.

> "They overcame him (the Devil) by the blood of the Lamb, and by the word of their testimony; and they loved not their lives unto the death." Revelation 12:11

Spiritual Warfare and the Blood Covenant are inexorably linked together. The lack of understanding of covenant and things of the Spirit, has resulted in weak Christian wrestlers. By understanding our covenant position in Jesus Christ, we can wage war against the enemies of the Cross from a position of strength. It is not our own natural strength, but the strength we receive through our relationship with

God. We are more than conquerors through Christ Jesus and we can do all things through him. When we understand our covenant position of reconciliation, the stage is set for spiritual conflict.

> "But when they have heard, Satan cometh immediately and taketh away the word that was sown in their hearts" (Mark 4:15)

When we have heard the Word of God or have received understanding concerning His Covenant, we must immediately wrestle to keep that truth. Satan does not want you to know what is yours. He knows that once you understand your contractual, covenant rights, you become dangerous to his plans and devices. He **must** come immediately and take it away or it will become rooted into our lives.

What Jesus did on the cross of Calvary has been hidden in covenant language and understanding. Our society has moved away from covenant understanding and we have, as a result, moved away from covenant power. Because of what Jesus did at Calvary and completed in His resurrection, and because of the enemy's determined to keep it from you, we are truly engaged in a Blood-War.

2
ARE YOU AN OVERCOMER

"They overcame him by the blood of the Lamb, and by the word of their testimony and they loved not their lives unto the death." Revelation 12:11

The life of the born-again Christian is not a life of simple ease. We have all experienced the day-to-day trials of life and have had to overcome negative circumstances that come our way. What we have just described would be considered, by many people, to be the daily problems of life. The task of maintaining our lives grows more burdensome, it would seem, with each generation.

A quick glance at the evening news tells us the that world in which we live is growing increasingly violent and hostile. The spirits of murder, perversion, lust, and greed, seemingly rule the streets of our nation. These spirits are prevalent as well in the high speed worlds of the financial, political, and social elite. Never before in history has the average person, young and old, been subjected to such a constant stream of violence and sensuality as today. This barrage comes mainly through the motion picture, television and printed media. Is it any wonder that principles of morality; such as virginity, chastity, abstinence, and purity are viewed as "victorian" and "prudish."

And yet the Bible still represents the principles that God has laid out for successful residence in the

Earth which He created. Just as an automobile comes from the factory with an owner's manual, God's Word is man's owner's manual for life. It contains all the necessary facts and principles which must be respected and adhered to in order to keep His creation from self-destruction. As is the case with an automobile, without an understanding of the basic principles of operation,(or by outright rejection of those principles) a driver will eventually destroy that vehicle - possibly causing injury to passengers and other drivers in the process.

The rejection and intellectual dismissal of the truths of God's Word by an "enlightened" society has resulted in the self-destruction of many institutions needed for its perpetuation, for example, the home, morality, and justice. With destruction comes confusion and an utter sense of hopelessness.

Into this confusion and despair, the Spirit-filled Christian is still sent in obedience to the "Great Commission."[a] It is the task of the followers of Jesus to invade this hostile environment with the "Good News" of God's love and mercy; which He displayed through the death and resurrection of Jesus. In order to be an effective witness to the saving grace of Jesus we must assume the posture of a warrior.

Nothing of value is achieved easily! Without the element of struggle and sacrifice, any achievement lacks a real sense of victory. As we achieve the

---

[a]. Mark 16:15

victory of sharing the Gospel in a hostile and rebellious society, we also sense the true nature of victory. In other words, the greater the battle; the greater the victory.

The rebellion and continuing conflict we live in today, began in heaven when Lucifer (one of the Archangels around God's throne) decided that he wanted God's glory. The very glory he was assigned to bring to the throne[a]. As a result, Lucifer was expelled from heaven and exiled to the earth. He is next found in the Garden of Eden, taking the form of a serpent, in order to deceive God's newly created man.

Some so called "scholars" would attempt to refute the existence of a personal devil (a.k.a. Satan and Lucifer). In order to support these false conclusions, one must refute the testimony of scripture and the character of Jesus Christ Himself. William Evans in his classic book on Bible Doctrines summarizes this logic and its fallacy when he says:

> "There can scarcely be any doubt as to the fact that Christ taught the existence of a personality of evil. There can be but three explanations as to the meaning of His teaching: First, that He accommodated His language to a gross superstition, knowing it to be such. If this be true then what becomes of His sincerity? Second, that He shared the

---

[a]. Isaiah 14:12-14; Revelation 12:7

superstition not knowing it to be such. Then what becomes of His omniscience, of His reliability as a teacher from God? Third, that the doctrine is not superstition, but actual truth. This position completely vindicates Christ as to His sincerity, omniscience and infallibility as the teacher sent from God."[a]

Satan and his angels are active in the everyday lives of humanity. There is indeed a personality of Evil. Scripture declares his activity and personality. We must accept the task of combatting him in our generation.

The conflict in which we must be engaged is not one with flesh and blood, as Paul declares, but it is a warfare in the spirit realm. Satan is called the "prince of the power of the air"[b] and the "god of this world."[c] He heads a kingdom which is hostile to the Kingdom of God and of Christ[d]. As believers, we have been translated through the new-birth into the Kingdom of God, therefore, Satan is hostile towards us.

We are placed, by the new nature within us, at odds with evil; and therefore at odds with the "evil one." Peter declares in 1 Peter 5:8 that he, the devil, is

---

[a]. The Great Doctrines of the Bible, William Evans, Moody Press, Chicago, 1912, revised 1974, pg.227
[b]. Ephesians 2:2
[c]. 2 Corinthians 4:4
[d]. Colossians 1:13

our adversary and he is seeking "whom he may devour." The devil is on an aggressive, evil pursuit; and has a strategy to deceive, oppress, and hinder the children of God in their efforts to be what God has called them to be. It is his intention to hinder what God has called them to do; evangelize the world.

3
TO GOD BE THE GLORY

The focus of Satan's attack is primarily on the Born-again, Spirit filled believer. The issue is still the same one which caused his exile from heaven - The Glory of God. Satan wanted what he could not have; God's glory. Because he could not have it, he has tried to establish himself as "the god of this world" in an attempt to receive glory from God's creation. As a result of this, there is an increase of open Satanic worship in our world today.

Many in the Rock and Roll music industry are bold to declare their allegiance to Satan and blatantly declare his praise in their lyrics. It is common knowledge that some recording artists have even dedicated their work to Satan in exchange for his "blessing" (really it's his curse). The worship of Satan is so commonplace that many of the comments of these "rockers" go relatively unnoticed. Satan, in his attempt to establish himself as a false deity, has found success and fame in the music and motion picture industry. The issue, however, is the Glory of God which He still desires with a vengeance.

Timothy M. Warner explains that the "modis operandi" of the devil is to bring deception and doubt to the Christian about his potential in Jesus Christ. Through the escalation of humanism, men and women are deceived into thinking that they are self-sufficient.

"The principle tactic of Satan in his

conflict with God from the very beginning, therefore, has been to deceive God's children into believing that the tremendous potential which resides within them can be realized by living life under their own control rather than under God's control and to believe that there is a legitimate source of power other than Yahweh. There is no doubt that this human creature made in the image of God had incredible potential. The humanists who say there are vast untapped resources within us are partly right. Satan was wise enough to recognize this, and he has been trying to sell the lie of humanism (i.e., we can achieve our full potential apart from a relationship with the Creator) in one form or another ever since his first encounter with Eve in the Garden."[a]

We are created in God's image in order to "show forth the praises of Him who has called you out of darkness."[b] We are called to be the "praise of His Glory."[c] In other words, it is the task of Christians to do all within their power, and the power that has been placed within them, to bring glory to God. God deserves all glory, honor and praise. Satan could not get God's glory, so his goal is to keep those

---

[a]. Spiritual Warfare, Victory over the Powers of World, Timothy M. Warner, Crossway Books, Wheaton, Il, 1991, pg.18
[b]. 1 Peter 2:9
[c]. Ephesians 1:12

who have been created in the image of God from bringing God glory.

Satan not only wants the credit for what God does; but he wants to place the blame for his activities at the throne of God, thereby receiving glory by default.

> "The Devil cannot deprive God of glory in Heaven, but he can keep God from having His rightful glory ascribed to Him by people on earth. He does this by keeping them blind to God's true character and to His purpose in creating and re-creating them and by keeping them ignorant of the power which is available to them to achieve that purpose. And when some of the people of earth do seek the Lord and try to walk in His ways, Satan can at least keep them from living in a manner that is "to the praise of His glory." The key in either case is to get them to live self-centered rather than God-centered lives, to buy into his lies about life, and to substitute Satan's kind of power for God's power."[a]

Lost Relationship

Through Satan's initial act of deception in the

---

[a]. Spiritual Warfare, pg.22

Garden of Eden, man was restricted from having the kind of relationship that he was intended to have with his heavenly Father. God had become man's Judge rather than his Friend. Sin had altered their divine relationship.

The strength of being in relationship with God as a Friend had been altered as death entered into man in fulfillment of God's promise concerning the fruit of the tree. Man did not immediately die, but spiritual death was immediate. The spirit of man which had been formed by the breath of God had become alienated from God because of sin[a]. Man and God had become estranged through the divorce of disobedience and spiritual death. Man could not be in relationship with God on an intimate level and remain in the earth[b].

The relationship which had been destroyed could only be restored through the establishment of a covenant which both parties agreed to. God was not without a plan. Immediately, upon judging the sin in the Garden, God makes a prophetic announcement concerning the "Seed of the Woman."[c] This is the first "cloaked' announcement of the ultimate victory that would come through Jesus Christ, the Seed of the woman.

We begin to see the mystery of redemption from this point of sin as well as open conflict with

---

[a]. Ephesians 2:12; Colossians 1:21
[b]. Genesis 5:24
[c]. Genesis 3:15

evil. It is a conflict which will progress through the Old Testament trail of covenant relationships. It will encompass multiple generations and crescendo in Jerusalem with the shedding of Jesus' blood at Calvary. God's declaration of the "crushing" of Satan's head is the battle cry of the Old Covenant. Starting in the Garden, we begin the ultimate battle between the plan of God; and the goal of the Evil One. The battle is: God's plan versus the determination of the devil. That is why we are engaged in Spiritual Warfare.

4
WHAT IS A COVENANT?

Covenant...the word literally means "to cut." It is a word that carries vast importance; but unfortunately, is not understood by most Christians. It would appear that the more casual the Christian, the more profound the ignorance of the meaning of covenant.

The understanding of covenant is a key factor in understanding the Bible. Ignorance of covenant has led to misunderstanding of scripture and erroneous doctrines that adulterate the character of God and leave the followers of these doctrines in defeat and discouragement. God is a covenant keeping God! His covenant integrity is what we count on when we trust in Him.

Webster's Dictionary defines covenant as," a solemn agreement". The Hebrew word for covenant means to "cut a compact" (because a covenant is made by a person passing between two pieces of cut flesh).[a] In its true definition, the word "covenant" surpasses the meaning of the words,"agreement" and "contract". It is a word of strength and power. The very character of the word demands respect.

Covenant is a solemn, serious, and binding contract between parties involving a cut. A covenant,

---

[a]. Strong's Concordance #1285 Hebrew & Chaldee Dictionary

simply stated, is an agreement or contract. In our society we enter into various covenants, or contracts and agreements, regularly. They are a part of our lives. A covenant can be entered into by simply giving someone your "word." In many cases in a court of law, a verbal contract can be as binding as a written one. Generally, we understand covenants to be no more than a contract or agreement.

Contractual Living

Many times in our lives we have lived under contract to an institution, person, or system. As a young man of 18 years old I came to believe that I would inevitably be drafted to serve in the military during the Vietnam War. I began to make tentative plans to avoid serving in the Army by joining the Marine Corp as my two older brothers had done. It was my plan to join the reserves and not be assigned combat duty, but to serve six months and then return to civilian life for all but one weekend a month. I did not make the final decision until July when my girlfriend and I had an argument and broke up.

Thinking that our relationship was over, I marched down to the Recruiter and signed a contract with the United States government. The agreement stated that I would serve in the Marines for at least six months starting in September.

A few days later Renee and I made up. July turned to August and President Nixon declared the draft discontinued. In its place the president instituted a lottery. My name and number were never drawn. I, nevertheless, was official property of the United States Marine Corps. That September I boarded a bus for San Diego and began basic training, knowing that a contract with the Marine Corps was indeed binding.

On another occasion, I signed a contract with a local bank to finance a beautiful car. I wanted the car and would have signed anything to get it. Sometime after signing the contract I found that my poor financial management resulted in my money being spent before all the bills were paid. I decided to just wait until next month and hopefully catch up. Next month came and the same management (rather, mismanagement) occurred and the same bills once more went unpaid.

The car was mine, or so I thought. At least until the bank notified me they would soon take their car back, if I did not live up to the terms of our agreement. The bank had agreed to let me use their car. I had agreed to reduce the amount financed on the car on a monthly basis. It was then that I realized that a contract with a lending institution was indeed binding.

Another incident involving the same shiny red Chevrolet, really drove home the point of contractual living to me. My "hot-rod" was equipped with a large V-8 engine, dual exhaust pipes and bucket seats. When you started the engine it would roar to life and vibrate with power. The speedometer pronounced that the top speed was 120 miles per hour.

Late one night after a date, I headed toward my home. The drive was approximately twenty miles of empty freeway. I looked down at the bluish green lighted instrument panel and the speedometer that implied that this "hot-rod" would move at 120 miles per hour. I looked at the empty freeway and decided to test the truth of what I believed. I pressed on the throttle pedal and my shiny red machine began to accelerate down the seemingly empty road. I watched as 65 miles per hour, the legal speed limit, was surpassed by 70 miles per hour, then 80, and then 90. I saw the indication that I had reached the speed of 110 miles per hour, when I noticed in my rear view mirror a car had come up onto the freeway. I quickly realized that the car behind me was also moving very fast. Immediately, I released the throttle pedal, allowing my car to slow to the legal speed limit, as I saw red lights appear on the rapidly approaching Highway Patrol car. The officer who stopped me, fervently reminded me, that when I signed the application for my drivers license I had agreed to drive within the legal speed limit. Although he consented to give me grace and only cite me for excessive speed, rather than reckless driving, upon facing the Judge, I learned that a contract with the State of California legal system is indeed binding.

What is Integrity

These three experiences illustrate examples of contracts under which we may find ourselves under in our life time. The extent to which we adhere to these agreements has a profound effect, at times, on the quality of our life. Those who know us, as well as those who wish to know about us, understand our ability to live within the framework of contracts and agreements as our integrity. If we have shown an unwillingness to abide by contracts in our lives, we are regarded as credit risks, un-bondable, and untrustworthy.

Integrity is then the strength of a contract. That strength is translated into power. Financial, social, political and spiritual power are the result of integrity in each respective area. Our ability or inability to live with integrity (keeping agreements) has a powerful impact on our lives. Success in spiritual warfare is greatly determined by the power of integrity.

With this in mind, we must understand that a covenant is more than just an agreement. It is a solemn contract. It has strength. It is something that is lived by and died for. The character of a covenant requires that it be adhered to and revered. The decision to enter into a covenant, therefore, should not be taken lightly or be under false pretenses. A covenant contains within it solemn and serious promises, provisions or vows. These vows contain the reason for the "cut" as well as the power that will be released through its fulfillment.

What is Marriage

The closest representation of the strength intended within covenant bonds is found in the marriage covenant. A marriage takes place when a man and a women wish to pledge themselves to each other for the rest of their natural lives. It is a special day when guests are invited and families are joined together. It is not a trivial thing when vows concerning life and death are shared.

In modern times the marriage covenant does not appear to contain lasting strength. Studies show that up to 60 percent of marriages, in America, end in divorce. But the purpose of the marriage in God's eyes has not changed. He intends for it to contain strength that will last until death. Because of the ignorance of covenant in our high paced, humanistic, and hedonistic society, the marriage covenant is taken much too lightly, resulting in broken relationships and shattered lives.

The vows of marriage are "till death do us part". Swearing until death is no laughing matter, especially when the power of God is evoked by a minister of the Gospel. Two hearts are united as a result of two people making covenant vows to each other in the presence of witnesses. God takes these vows very seriously. We are told by the Apostle Paul that the marriage bed is undefiled, however, God will judge those who corrupt those vows[a].

Consider the vows that are traditionally shared at the marriage altar.
"Till death do us part"
"I promise to love, cherish, etc."
"All my worldly goods I thee endow"
"Keeping myself only unto you"

---

[a] Hebrews 13:4

Each of these vows are witnessed and agreed to by each party and their invited guests. At the conclusion of making vows to each other, the minister administers the proclamation, "I pronounce you man and wife, in the name of the Father, The Son, and the Holy Ghost." As the pronouncement is made, the power of God to seal those vows is evoked when he says, "In the name of the Father, Son and Holy Ghost." God witnesses and seals those vows. In other words, the couple has not only made vows to each other; but have made vows to God. His emissary declares it a marriage and says, "Amen."

This familiar example of covenant, which I have just discussed, is representative of the seriousness of making vows and entering into covenant relationship. While a simple contract deals primarily with physical things, a covenant affects spiritual, emotional, as well as finite, temporal, and physical things. A covenant by it's nature is not to be taken lightly.

In the marriage covenant the vows which are made are sacred promises. The typical church wedding has all the elements of an ancient covenant ceremony. The two families join together in a predetermined meeting place. The two families represented sit on different sides while the covenant is negotiated. The parents and family patriarchs sit up close where they can best observe and give their agreement to the union that will take place.

The groom is always adorned, second only to the bride who is the center piece of the ceremony. All effort has been taken to beautify and perfect the appearance of both the bride and the groom before presenting them to the priest or minister at this gathering of family and guests. These two are the representation of the respective parents, their family, and everything that is characteristic of each family. These two individuals are always presented in the best light for they declare the image of the parents.

As the anticipation builds, God's representative, the minister, steps to center stage and awaits the arrival of the bride and groom. The groom enters first to await his beloved, who will be ushered in by the head of the family, or the patriarch of the bride's family. As they meet before the minister, they are in essence meeting at the altar of God. They stand between both families and before God who will give the final "amen" to their union.

The minister calls the meeting to attention as he explains the reason for coming together, the joining of these two individuals in the holy estate of marriage. He asks if there is any one that knows of any reason why the two cannot become one. Is there any sin or defilement, or insincerity that would result in a false union?

After a silence that is considered as consent, the minister leads the two in marriage covenant vows. There is a mutual exchange of assets as they declare, "with all my worldly goods I thee endow". The covenant vows are sealed with (the promise of) death being the only agency of division that will be tolerated.

After an exchange of tokens of the covenant they are pronounced man and wife. The token is represented in the golden rings which are given by the groom to the bride and vis a versa. The ring is symbolic of two raised welts or scars that will represent the fact that they have entered into a covenant relationship with a member of the opposite sex till death.

After the pronunciation of the union of covenant, the two retreat down the alley or isle between the two families and invite them to the covenant feast or reception. Here the two families begin to intermingle and become friends. During the course of the reception, celebration is made for the joining of these two people who have become one by joining their strengths and weaknesses together in a covenant relationship.

After a time the bride and groom are released to culminate their union in what we call the "honeymoon." If both individuals have retained their virginity until this sacred night of emotional and physical union, they will experience the shedding of blood in the process of joining their bodies together. (We will deal with this powerful exchange later and we will see that God has intended an awesome truth to be evident.)

In its intended purity, the marriage becomes a powerfully significant exchange of covenant blessing and mutual devotion. It should not be taken lightly. God is a covenant keeping God and He will release His power on behalf of a marriage when faith and obedience to Him, and our vows, is reverently displayed.

The marriage covenant is only one of the covenants in which we become involved in ours lives. It is, however, a good representation of the sacredness and severity of the nature of covenant. God initiated the marriage covenant. We will see that God is the originator of covenant principle, the one who has determined its severity, and the one who empowers the principles involved in covenant.

Whenever men become involved in covenant, whether purposefully or ignorantly, God has placed within the covenant a power that can, and will, bring blessing and cursing into the lives of those involved. Whether a covenant provides blessing or cursing is determined by the purpose of the covenant and the level of adherence to its principles.

5
TWO TYPES OF COVENANTS

Primarily, we are acquainted with contract type covenants as with the example of the marriage vows. However, when examining covenants in the Bible we see two types of covenants: unilateral and bilateral.

Unilateral Covenants

A unilateral covenant is a solemn vow that you make with yourself. These types of covenants do not require the participation of another, nor are they contingent on the performance of any prerequisite action. It is the promise in the form of a serious vow that a person makes without condition. This type of covenant is what we would make when we make a New Years resolution or we tell ourself that we will lose weight or begin some sort of discipline. We make a solemn vow of dedication.

Bilateral Covenants

A bilateral agreement is what we non attorneys commonly understand as a contract. Two or more parties involved in the fulfillment of a contract, which is dependent on both parties for conditions of completion constitutes a bilateral contract or covenant. The marriage covenant best exemplifies what is known as a bilateral covenant. In other words the two parties mutually exchange vows and agree to the terms.

As you will see throughout our study, the Old and New Covenants are in fact bilateral in nature.

Where It All Began

God, who created all things, is the originator of covenant. Adam and Eve's act of disobedience in Genesis chapter three resulted in them being expelled from the Garden and, more importantly, from intimate relationship with the Creator. God commands a curse on the serpent and declares that the seed of the woman will bruise, or crush the head of the serpent. This constitutes a unilateral covenant. God said in essence, "I make a vow unto myself." (The promise which God made in the Garden was, of course, cloaked in a mystery which would be revealed later[a]).

In making this serious declaration, God, in fact, bound Himself to a unilateral covenant. His covenant vow and its fulfillment was not dependent on man's performance or lack of performance. It had no requirement of righteousness. It would simply be fulfilled by God in the ages to come.

This covenant, made by God with Himself, would set the stage for the redemption of us all. God's covenant was to be the salvation of His man. In Adam's sinful state he could not be responsible for the fulfillment of God's covenant. God called this "My covenant." Later, in scripture we see God refer to this covenant, when He speaks to man in His dealings

---

[a]. 1 Corinthians 2:7,8

with the earth.

We find in Genesis chapter six that man became so corrupt that God repents that He made him.[a] God declares that He will destroy man from off the Earth. Noah, however, finds favor with the Lord and is positioned to be spared. The Lord declares that He will establish HIS Covenant with Noah.

> "But with thee I will establish my covenant; and thou shalt come into the ark, thou, and thy sons, and thy wife, and thy son's wives with thee." (Genesis 6:18)

"His" Covenant is the unilateral covenant He made when pronouncing that the Seed of the Woman would crush the head of the serpent. He tells Noah that He will continue to honor the vow that He made for the "Seed" of the Woman. The total elimination of man from the earth would make the fulfillment of the vow impossible.

The vow which God made was declared in the ears of Satan, as well as Adam and Eve. By saying, "the Seed of the Woman" it was understood that the seed would be an heir of Adam and Eve. Recreation of the race of man would violate the promise made in the ears of those present. Therefore, Noah would be the fulfillment of God's unilateral covenant vow. God would "establish" HIS Covenant with Noah and so the woman's seed would be preserved.

---

[a] Genesis 6:6

Another beautiful example of a unilateral covenant is found in Genesis chapter nine. After the destruction, God promises He will never destroy the earth by flood again. He refers to His promise as the "Covenant between He and the earth;"[a] The token of that covenant would be the colorful bow in the sky.

---

[a]. verse 13

6
WHERE POWER COMES FROM

When God created the heavens and the earth he initiated and ordained certain natural laws. These laws have within them power. This power is the strength of these laws. Let's use for an example the law of gravity.

This law works on all objects on the earth. Its power is expressed when we jump up, or in any way attempt to release ourselves from confines of the earth. When we operate in agreement with the law of gravity, we can experience the blessing of its power. What would basketball be like if there were no Law of gravity? Imagine trying to bounce a ball that had no pull of gravity on it. Consider the hardship a lack of gravity would produce on shooting for a basket. This simple illustration shows how we benefit from the blessings of the power within the law of gravity.

We know what happens when we attempt to act in disagreement with the law of gravity. Any sky diver knows that the parachute is designed to counteract the force of gravity that would invariably pull him to his death when he jumped out of a plane. If the parachute fails, the power of gravity would then be a curse rather than a blessing.

Science and scientists are constantly at work discovering what blessings can be had when acting in harmony with natural law. Where those laws seem to hinder the efforts of the scientist an attempt must be made to somehow circumvent or supersede those laws. The discovery of the laws of lift and thrust allows us to build airplanes that fly high and fast. The law of gravity is thereby superseded by the more dominant physical laws, which allows flight.

God has given us His book, The Bible, to bring understanding of natural laws as well the spiritual laws. Many scientists and inventors have found the answers to questions concerning the natural forces of the earth from the pages of Scripture.

While on a sick bed, Matthew Fontaine Maury, discovered the Bible's account of "paths in the sea"[a]. "If there are paths in the sea, I am going to find them when I get out of this bed," he declared to his son.

Maury became the first to recognize the interaction of the earth's winds upon the currents of the sea. From this, he reasoned that there must be paths beneath the sea that would permit ships to make better time if they took advantage of these natural undersea "routes".

From ship's logs he studied these natural laws of winds and currents in detail, then plotted ship routes across the ocean that later became the basis of an international maritime agreement. In 1923, Muary's home state of Virginia erected monuments both in Richmond and in Goshen that pay tribute to Muary's achievements; but not to the part the Bible

---

[a]. Psalms 8:8

played in his discoveries. The inscription on one of those monuments reads in part:

> "Matthew Fontaine Muary, pathfinder of the seas, the genius who first snatched from the ocean the secret of their laws...Every mariner for countless ages, as he takes his chart to shape his course through the seas, will think of thee."[a]

Maury discovered how to use the power of sea currents for blessing. Prior to his discovery they were considered restrictions and "course disruptive" curses.

Natural Law and Spiritual Law

As surely as God created natural law, he also created and ordained spiritual laws or principles. These laws act the same as the natural laws in that they retain power that is released when acted on. The laws are spiritual forces that are as real and vital as the natural laws we live with. The fact that we don't see them or accept them does not eliminate their existence. Many of mankind's problems can be traced to a violation of a spiritual law. Because God is a Spirit[b], we can expect these spiritual laws to be the more powerful than even natural laws. These laws are filled with God's power.

When you violate a spiritual law, the effects are often not seen instantly. However, if the violation

---

[a]. The Book of Fascinating Christian Facts, Robert Flood, Accent Books, Denver CO. 1985 p.154
[b]. John 4:24

persists, the ultimate consequence will exceed the violation of natural law. For example, if you sit on a second story window ledge and carelessly slip off, falling to the ground below; you will immediately "pay a fine" to the law of gravity; that of a sprained or broken back.

When you violate a spiritual law such as "love your neighbor, as yourself," there is initially minimum effect. However, whether you act ignorantly or intentionally, you have set a spiritual law into motion. If there is no correction, the ultimate end will be a disaster ranging from a broken relationship to, in the extreme case, "He who lives by the sword, dies by the sword." In the event of the later, you may pay the ultimate "fine"; eternal damnation.

The Law of Agreement

The power of agreement is one of these spiritual laws. It is a powerful force when men enter into covenant relationship.   Agreement is the necessary force used in the establishment of bilateral covenants. This force is released and empowers that "contract."

Before a bilateral covenant can become effective, both parties must consent or agree. The agreement becomes the legal and moral strength of that union. If, after an agreement has been reached and the covenant is sealed, either party comes to disagree with the terms of the covenant; and begins to display that disagreement by failing to fulfill their covenant obligations, there is a "breach". If the covenant included an enforcement clause, that covenant immediately begins to work against whichever party is in disagreement.

In the event of a breach of covenant, the strength of the agreement works in reverse as a curse. In other words, although the covenant agreement was intended as a means to blessing, its breach causes its strength to work against the covenant breaker. What was then intended to be a friend has become an enemy.

You can see then that the originator of the covenant is not bringing the curse; but rather, the one who breaks the covenant agreement is in fact unleashing covenant power in a negative manner. Many times what has been interpreted as a curse is nothing more than a "blessing" in reverse.

The reason for coming together in covenant agreement, is usually for positive results. That is to say, two people have a mutual interest for forming an agreement. The power of agreement is than by nature; positive. God's kingdom is also by nature; positive. He has empowered the principles of covenant for the purpose of positive relationships. His desire is that we live in covenant agreement and walk in blessing.

Because the very nature of our adversary is negative, he wants to be covenant breakers, so that the negative characteristics of the power of agreement are unleashed into our lives.

Satan has been defeated by the death, burial, and resurrection of Jesus Christ. Jesus declares, "All power in heaven and in earth are Mine". Satan cannot create anything or any power, because he is not God. He is limited to using that which was designed and intended for our good, and by enlisting our disobedience, reverse it and make it a curse. The devil uses covenant power against us by enticing us to break God's laws. When we live in violation of His laws, those same laws work against us.

The Apostle Paul tells us, concerning the covenant meal, which we know as Communion, that we can bring a sentence or condemnation upon ourselves; if we don't discern the Lord's body[a]. If we go through the expression of covenant, the partaking of the bread and cup, without comprehending the ramifications of covenant power; Paul says, we will be among those who are weak and sickly and even die prematurely. The power of agreement with Christ's death and life, while intended to be for salvation, will then become our damnation.

While many may reject the idea that the blood and body of Jesus could in any way become a "curse", the fact is that failure to accept Jesus' sacrifice and submit to the power of that blood and body will result in eternal alienation from God; and eternal punishment for the very sins Jesus sacrificed Himself to forgive. So while the greatest gift to mankind was intended for our good, our rejection of it, or our

---

[a]. 1 Corinthians 11:29

violation of it, causes the gift to be our judge. Hell will be filled with the remembrance of the power in the Blood of Jesus Christ and the covenant it represents.

7
STRATEGY FOR VICTORY

The most wonderful example of the power of agreement is seen in the compound unity of the Godhead. "God, in three persons, blessed Trinity." Unity and agreement always release power.[a]

For this reason, God initiated the principles of covenant. When agreement is present a power is released into the earth. When covenants are instituted for the wrong reasons there is still power released. The "Costa Nostra" operates in blood covenant. Although the purpose is for the propagation of evil and criminal behavior, the same power is released - the power of agreement. It is especially interesting to note that those who enter the mafia through a covenant of blood are afforded all the strength of the "Godfather".

When God pronounced His Covenant in the Garden, power was released to cause it to happen. Eternity could not resist the magnitude of God's plan. Nothing could stop the covenant of grace and mercy from being fulfilled once the Almighty spoke it. God, in agreement with Himself (in "unilateral" covenant) would produce the ultimate victory.

Immediately, upon the pronouncement of His Covenant, God began to express it through similitude, and types, and shadows. God's first act was the

---

[a]. Matthew 18:19

covering of man's nakedness through the shedding of blood. An animal was sacrificed in order to provide man's covering for sin. Because man had sinned against God, only God could initiate a covering. Man can never cover his own sin against God. Any attempt to do so results in failure and added disgrace. A lie covered by a lie only serves to compound the sin.

We see later, in the sacrifices of Cain and Abel, the institution of an offering of blood. Abel offered unto God an acceptable sacrifice of an animal. Obviously, sometime prior to this time, the institution of animal sacrifice had been ordained. We see the same institution when Noah comes out of the ark. There, he offers an animal sacrifice unto the Lord. The institution of animal sacrifice pointed toward the fulfillment of God's covenant. God would ultimately offer the supreme sacrifice of His son, the Lamb of God.

The effect of man's original sin was devastating. Man could no longer be in the same intimate fellowship with his Creator. Sin had caused a separation. Man became simply a servant, subject to the elements around him and subservient to the power of sin.[a] Man's delegated authority had been given to Satan through Adam's disobedience[b]. Man became the ruled, instead of the ruler, and sin would have dominion over God's man until Calvary.

---

[a]. Galatians 4:7,8
[b]. Luke 4:6

Hebrews tells us that Man's sin also affected the heavenly tabernacle. Moses's tabernacle was only an earthly representation of the one which exists in heaven.

> "In the same way, he (Moses) sprinkled with blood both the tabernacle and everything used in its ceremonies. In fact, the law requires that nearly everything be cleansed with blood; and without the shedding of blood there is no forgiveness. It was necessary, then, for the copies of the heavenly things to be purified with these sacrifices; but the heavenly things themselves with better sacrifices than these. For Christ did not enter a man-made sanctuary that was only a copy of the true one; he entered heaven itself, now to appear for us in God's presence."
> Hebrews 9:21 - 24 NIV

Now we can understand why Jesus, upon meeting Mary at the tomb immediately after His resurrection, told her not to touch Him for He had not ascended to His Father[a]. Later, upon meeting His disciples, He instructs Thomas to handle Him to prove He had risen from the dead. Jesus ascended and cleansed the heavenly tabernacle between His meeting with Mary and His meeting with Thomas.

---

[a]. John 20:17

Man's sin had alienated him from God, and God from him. Because man had caused the separation, man had to be involved with the restoration. However, man could not redeem himself because his sin was against God; therefore, God also had to initiate the reconciliation. Redemption must be initiated by the greater to the lesser. The weak cannot approach the strong unless a way is made. Man could not approach God in His sin. A cover would be needed.

The significance of blood as a covering agent is due to the fact that it represents life[a]. When sin entered man's spirit, so did death. Death has been lodged in man from the original sin of Adam[b]. The blood then is symbolic of life being the conqueror of death. However, the blood of animals was insufficient in that it could not remove the sin of man. Institution of animal blood sacrifice could only act as a covering for sin, an atonement for sin[c].

God's Covenant Crisis

In Genesis chapter six we read that man had become evil in his thoughts, and so wicked that God "repented" that He had made man. God was grieved because of man's perpetuation and escalation of sin. It would seem that God would have to start over. The Lord said, "I will destroy man whom I have created from the face of the earth; both man, and beast, and

---

[a]. Deuteronomy 12:23 "...for the blood is the life.."
[b]. Romans 5:12
[c]. Hebrews 10:4

creeping thing, and the fowls of the air; for it repenteth me that I made them."ᵃ

But the Lord found a man named Noah, a just man who lived in a manner pleasing unto God. Because God had made His covenant concerning the seed of the woman, and had made that vow in the presence of the devil and all of His creation, God needed a "seed" in the earth to fulfill his vow.

The Lord said to Noah, "But with thee I will establish My Covenantᵇ". Here the Lord is referring to the unilateral covenant He made in the Garden as "My Covenant". Notice, He did not say that Noah would be involved in that covenant. No conditions of performance were dictated. God only said He would establish His Covenant with Noah. The Hebrew word that is interpreted "establish", is a word that can also mean "continue". In other words the statement could be interpreted, "I will continue My Covenant with thee".

It is an accepted doctrinal principle that "God changes not." God has never changed and the covenant that is referred to in the preservation of Noah is God's Covenant, which He made saying, "The Seed of the woman would crush the serpents head." Noah would serve as the generational line through whom the fulfillment of God's covenant would continue.

---

[a] Genesis 6:7
[b] Genesis 6:18 italics mine

This reference to "My Covenant" is not to be mistaken, however, for the covenant that God made with the earth when he promised to never again destroy the earth with water. This covenant was sealed with a "bow' in the sky. Each time we see a "rainbow" we are reminded again that God is a covenant keeping God.

God's Strategy and Abram

God's covenant is kept a mystery throughout the first eleven chapters of Genesis as Noah's family leaves the ark and a new civilization is formed. The only other mention of covenant in these chapters occurs when Noah leaves the ark. God makes a covenant with the earth and says it is "a covenant" in which a bow is placed in the clouds as a token[a].

However, in Genesis, chapter twelve we find a change in the relationship God will have with His man. Abram is called out of Ur of the Chaldees and is directed toward a promised land. In the process of calling Abram out, God promises to bless him and make a great nation out of him. In chapter fifteen God makes another covenant statement to Abram. Notice the language, it speaks that this is "a covenant" with Abram. The language once again speaks of a "unilateral covenant". The promise connected to this "unilateral covenant" with Abram was that God would give unto Abram the land from the river of Egypt to the great river Euphrates. Again God does not put

---

[a]. Genesis 9:13

requirements on Abram at this time. He only makes a covenant to give Abram the land.

God was ready now to invite a man into covenant relationship with Him. Abram had been obedient in answering the call of God, and had positioned himself as a believer. Romans chapter four explains how Abram's faith was accounted unto him as righteousness.[a] The time had come to call on Abram to perform as a condition of covenant.

Genesis chapter seventeen begins with the account of God's appearance to Abram when he was ninety-nine years old. His statement to Abram is, "I am Almighty God; walk before me and be perfect". This statement is unique in that it initiates a conditional relationship between God and Abram. In verse four, God continues by saying, "As for me, behold, My Covenant is with thee..." God again refers to a pre-existing covenant known as "My Covenant". God is inviting Abram to enter into a conditional "bilateral" covenant. The covenant in which Abram is asked to participate is God's covenant of "crushing the serpent's head." In verse seven, new language is expressed concerning this new relationship. The Lord says, "I will establish (continue) My covenant between me and thee and thy seed after thee in their generations for an everlasting covenant, to be a God unto thee and to thy seed after thee." Nowhere prior has God used the word "between" when referring to His covenant. Abram's name is changed to Abraham,

---

[a]. Romans 4:22

reflecting the change in nature and relationship with God (just as a woman's name is changed to reflect her marriage). The epistle of Paul to the Galatians tells us that this promise, which included Abraham's seed, actually was referring to Jesus[a].

Abraham's condition for maintaining covenant relationship with Almighty God was to walk in perfection. God needed a man to begin the instruction in righteousness so that his seed could fulfill the standard and become the "serpent crusher". Abraham accepted the offer and his faith was imputed to him as righteousness, or "right-standing".

As this new covenant relationship was one between God and a man in the earth, whatever would be done in the earth would have to involve the man; as long as he met the covenant conditions. Because God dealt with Abraham as a friend, He could correct him "one-on-one". If Abraham violated his covenant responsibilities, God would come rebuke him and restore him to perfection.

The first "test" of this new covenant relationship is found in Genesis chapter eighteen. The Lord decided that the abominable acts being perpetrated in Sodom and Gomorrah would require the destruction of those cities. Because God had made a covenant relationship with Abraham, He would have to involve Abraham in the decision. In verse seventeen, in the Amplified Bible it reads, "And the Lord said, shall I

---

[a]. Galatians 3:16

hide from Abraham [My friend and servant] what I am about to do?" It goes on to say in verses eighteen and nineteen that He cannot hide it because He has made covenant promises to Abraham. It is Abraham who pleads for the righteous in the cities and negotiates with God concerning the destruction of Sodom and Gomorrah.

One of the most humorous and poignant accounts of man's right-standing with God and his ability to plead the case of humanity from a position of covenant righteousness is seen in this chapter. Abraham starts with the statement, "shall not the Judge of all the earth do right?" He begins with the arbitrary amount of fifty righteous and negotiates God down to ten. As you read this passage you begin to see the strength that comes through being in covenant with God. Abraham stands before God and basically says, "God, You will not destroy the righteous with the wicked, because You are the righteous Judge who must do right according to covenant." Here is a man in righteousness (right-standing) with God, talking with God, as an advocate before the Father in the affairs of men in the earth.

This account speaks loud and clear concerning the strength of God's covenant relationship with Abraham, through God's refusal to act in regards to Sodom and Gomorrah without first talking with His covenant man. The covenant relationship which Abraham had with God produced a righteousness, or "right-standing" with God that allowed him to dictate the articles of destruction or salvation of a city. God has placed within covenant relationship the ability of a man in righteousness to "stand in the gap" for his city, state or nation.

Covenant relationship is the strongest relationship on earth. Its gravity demands integrity, sincerity, and sobriety. God has put power in covenant and that power is to be respected and revered. God will honor and respect His covenant and all who enter into it.

8
GOD OF ABRAHAM, ISAAC & JACOB

"And I will establish my covenant between me and thee and thy seed after thee in their generations for an everlasting covenant, to be a God unto thee, and to thy seed after thee.

This is My covenant, which ye shall keep, between me and you and thy seed after thee; Every man child among you shall be circumcised." Genesis 17:7,10

The covenant relationship between God and Abraham was to be a relationship that also extended to Abraham's seed. This covenant would also have a seal of blood incorporated into it. Blood always represents life. By sealing this new covenant relationship through his blood by the act of circumcision, Abraham was sealing it with his life. The force of this blood covenant would be the added power of "blood-life". In other words Abraham was pledging his life to keep and maintain this covenant agreement with Almighty God. God is a spirit and therefore cannot shed blood in sealing this covenant. Man would pledge that which is most dear - his life.

Why Circumcision

Abraham also pledged the life of all his seed as he agreed to the terms of this covenant. Every descendent of Abraham would declare their allegiance by following Abraham in the ritual of circumcision. The cutting of the foreskin would carry implied significance in two ways.

One, the cutting of the foreskin of the penis placed the scar of covenant in the male reproductive organ. This is symbolic of sealing all of Abraham's seed into the covenant, even before they were to come out of his loins. Every seed of Abraham, whether male or female, would have to pass through the covenant made with God in order to be born in the earth.

Second, by placing the seal of covenant on the male sexual organ, God was making a statement about the value of virginity and the sacredness of marriage. Every male born child of Abraham would be required to place a holy standard on sex and marriage. Whenever a covenant man, sealed in the circumcision, was to enter into a marriage relationship, he was to find a woman who was a virgin. (In Deuteronomy 22:13 - 21 we read about the "tokens of virginity"). On the wedding night, the newlywed couple would be taken to a bed chamber that had been prepared by the bride's family. There they would consummate their marriage.

The next day the bride's parents would collect the bed sheets which were to have the tokens of her virginity. In the process of consummating the marriage through the act of sexual intercourse, the bride, a virgin, would shed blood caused by the penetration of the hymen membrane. These drops of blood would remain on the bed sheets, and were a record of her virtue prior to marriage.

The husband, who was a "son of Abraham", had placed in his members the scar of covenant. As he consummates the marriage, his bride's blood covers the covenant seal. The marriage is sealed and the covenant of Abraham is re-sealed at the same time. In this simple placement of the covenant scar, the circumcision, God made a powerful statement about the woman's place in covenant with her husband; while also making a strong statement concerning the value of virginity and the sacredness of the marriage bed.

Young men and women have been "brainwashed" by a promiscuous society that casual sex is a way of life; a culturally accepted norm. God does not agree! Sex is still intended for the holiness of marriage only. Once again the ignorance of covenant seems to have led us astray. Young people should be taught the covenant reason for virginity and purity. Fear of pregnancy, AIDS, and venereal disease has proved to be a very poor deterrent to sexual activity among our youth. God knew what he was doing when he made male and female. He called it very good[a]. He honors sex and marriage through the placement of the circumcision in the foreskin of the man.

Abraham's Blessing

---

[a]. Genesis 1:31

When Abraham entered into covenant with God through the circumcision of the flesh, God promised to bless Abraham. The conditions for walking in those blessings was absolute obedience and faith in his body and spirit. The statement, "Walk before me and be perfect" signifies that God expected Abraham to be in relationship with Him (walk before me), and that Abraham would obey without compromise (be thou perfect).

God promises to be a "God" unto Abraham and his seed. He announces Himself to Abraham as "El Shadai" or "Almighty God". God declares Himself to Abram in Genesis 17:1 as everything that Abram needs. "Almighty", meaning able to do all that Abram needs done. "God", meaning that which is supreme and the creative force of the universe.

Almighty God invited Abram to participate in a close "one-on-one" relationship which would cause the power of God to be at the disposal of a covenant man, while the power of the man was at the disposal of a covenant God. This man's obedience and faith would open the door for all might and power to be available to all who would walk in his example. Later, in Israel's history, we see men call fire out of heaven, raise the dead, stop the rotation of the earth; and even cause the earth to spin backwards with the might and power of God working with them in covenant relationship. The promise to "be a God unto thee" is evident throughout the story of the Bible.

Although the condition of perfection may seem stringent through our eyes. God knew that if

Abraham would only believe, it would allow them to cooperate and relate as friends. God could correct and adjust Abraham whenever necessary, if only Abraham would respond in faith to the initial offer. With his faith as his righteousness, Abraham entered into Adam's relationship with God and they became friends. Together with Abraham, God would fulfil His covenant to bring the "serpent crusher" into the earth. The promised seed would be the seed of Abraham.

As part of the promise He made with Abram (Abraham), God also promised to give Abram and Sarai a son whose name would be Isaac. Sarah, (formerly Sarai) was barren and 90 years old; but, God promised that she would conceive and bear a "son of promise".

It took twenty-five years for the fulfillment of the promise of Isaac. Sarah, in her frustration and impatience, encouraged Abraham to take Hagar, Sarah's maidservant, and produce a child. This son was Ishmael. Ishmael would become the beginning of a group of people generally known as Arabians. God's promise to bless Ishmael[a] is evident when we realize that the major control of the oil wealth of the world is in the hands of the Arabian sons of Ishmael. While Sarah attempted to produce the promise of God through natural means, Abraham's relationship of blessing was also passed on to Ishmael. God is a covenant keeping God.

---

[a]. Genesis 17:20

Many a promise from God has been missed by the impatience of men. God will keep His covenant promises. Men produce an "Ishmael" which remains as a testimony of their doubt and impatience. God, on the other hand will always produce the "Son of Promise". God's ways are always higher and more efficient than our ways.

Three Patriarchs

Isaac was the one whom God had promised to "perform" His covenant through[a]. In Genesis 26:3, the Lord appears to Isaac, now a man with a wife and children, and restates the promise He made with Abraham.

> "And the Lord appeared unto him and said...'Sojourn in this land, and I will be with thee, and I will bless thee; for unto thee and thy seed, I will give all these countries, and I will perform the oath which I sware unto Abraham thy father; and I will make thy seed to multiply as the stars of heaven, and will give unto thy seed all these countries; and in thy seed shall all the nations of the earth be blessed; because that Abraham obeyed my voice, and kept my charge, my commandments, my statutes, and my laws." (Genesis 26:2-5)

---

[a]. Genesis 17:19

Isaac was then invited into a cooperative covenant relationship with God in fulfilling the oath that He had made to his father Abraham. The terms would remain the same as with Abraham. God would once again deal with Isaac as a friend, one on one.

It is interesting to note that in the fulfilling of the covenant made with his father, Isaac even duplicated the error of lying to Abimelech, the king of the Philistines, concerning Rebekah, his wife. He tells the same lie in saying that Rebekah is his sister; truly, his father's son.

Isaac and Rebekah had two sons, Esau and Jacob. As a result of deception, Jacob inherits Isaac's blessing. This qualifies Jacob to be invited into the covenant relationship between God and Abraham and Isaac. We see this in Genesis 35:9 - 13.

The God of Abraham and Isaac became the God of Abraham, Isaac and Jacob. The covenant to send a "Serpent Crusher" was continued through the relationships of these three patriarchs. Each patriarch was a personal covenant representative of what God intended to do in the process of bringing forth a redeemer of all mankind.

9
THE RENEWED COVENANT

God changes not, neither has His covenant plan and purpose. The nation of Israel is formed through the faith and covenant agreements of Abraham, Isaac and Jacob. Through Jacob's twelve sons, the twelve tribes of Israel would be established and the story of the Old Testament would continue.

Because of Joseph's slavery and subsequent exaltation in Egypt. The nation or family of Israel is relocated to Egypt, where they eventually become slaves to the Pharaohs. The task masters of Egypt become harsh and abusive to the Hebrews. Joseph had died and the children of Israel began to cry out because of their bondage.

God heard their cry[a]. The statement on Exodus 2:24 is very clear as to why God raised up Moses to deliver the children of Israel out of Egypt. God is a covenant keeping God. Moses through the mighty power of God leads Israel out of Egypt and toward the promised land. The land that God promised to Abraham when he invited Abraham into "His" covenant.

However, at this time there were approximately two million Hebrew children coming out of Egypt. There had been four generations since Joseph relocated his father Jacob and the sons of Israel to

---

[a]. Exodus 2:23 - 25

Egypt. It would appear that the Children of Israel, for the most part, had forgotten the promise that God had made to Abraham. Over the long period of slavery, they apparently had not been taught what it meant to "walk before God and be perfect". But God remembered His covenant with Abraham and raised up Moses as a type and shadow of our redeemer Jesus.

Whether or not we remember covenant vows, God does not forget. He remembers covenant. He will honor those that honor covenant. The Lord had "respect" for Israel because of the relationship he had with Abraham Isaac and Jacob and brought them out of bondage with a mighty display of His power.

Because the population of Israel had grown over the past four generations since Joseph; and because the terms of the covenant was to be adhered to with "perfection" - the Lord had to renew His covenant with the entire Hebrew nation. No longer could He simply deal with a man as He had with Abraham, Isaac and Jacob. He would now deal with a nation of people called Israel.

In order to judge them with fairness and severity the Lord would have to give them a set of instructions and laws of conduct. If Israel was to "walk before God and be perfect", the nation must know and understand exactly what that meant. God would have to write His conditions so that the nation could agree to them. The Lord would put his "Tables of Covenant" in the hands of Moses for the people to read and obey.

Once Moses received the "Law" from the Lord, he read it to the people. All the people of Israel were present at the reading. A solemn decision would be needed at the end of the reading. Israel would then decide if they would renew the covenant of Abraham, Isaac and Jacob.

> "And Moses came and told the people all the words of the Lord, and all the judgements: and all the people answered with one voice, and said, All the words which the Lord hath said will we do. And Moses wrote all the words of the Lord, and rose early in the morning, and built an altar under the hill, and twelve pillars, according to the twelve tribes of Israel. And he sent young men of the children of Israel, which offered burnt offerings, and sacrificed peace offerings of oxen unto the Lord. And Moses took half of the blood and put it in basons; and half of the blood he sprinkled on the altar. And he took the book of the covenant, and read in the audience of the people; and they said, All that the Lord hath said will we do, and be obedient. And Moses took the blood, and sprinkled it upon the people, and said, Behold the blood of the covenant which the Lord has made with you concerning the all these words." (Exodus 24:3 - 8)

Moses referred to this act as a covenant of

blood. Israel renewed the Lord's Covenant[a]. The Lord called heaven and earth to record that day against the nation of Israel that He had placed before them life and death and blessings and cursing but they had chose life[b].

Renewed Relationship

We see in Deuteronomy 9:11 a statement that makes us understand the importance of the law which the Lord gave to Moses. We know that God's plan of redemption began in the Garden; and that He never altered his plan from the beginning[c], the statement "Tables of the Covenant" must mean the covenant that the Lord made for the redemption of man. God did not create a new set of standards for the nation of Israel. He simply wrote down the original standard, gave it to Moses, who read it to the people. When they agreed to all that the Lord had said, it became the Law. The Covenant of Abraham Isaac and Jacob was now the "Law" of Israel.

This set of Laws has governed the basic morality of all mankind ever since. The "Ten Commandments" are simply a part of the covenant. Men and women who will obey the commandments will find Gods blessing on them. God is our covenant keeping God. He still honors this Abrahamic and Mosaic Covenant. Just look at Israel today and those nations that maintain the standards of God. You will find them blessed. When nations reject the moral

---

[a]. Deuteronomy 30:20
[b]. Deuteronomy 30:19
[c]. Ephesians 3:3

standard of God, curses await them. Nations fall and rise because of the power of God's covenant and men's acceptance or rejection of it.

10
VICTORY THROUGH RELATIONSHIP

The question may be asked, "Is there a man in the Old Testament that used the Covenant of God on purpose. The nation of Israel was led out of Egypt because God "remembered" his Covenant with Abraham Isaac and Jacob. But there is no specific account where Moses used the covenant on purpose. There is a good example of a covenant minded man who lived His life and experienced victory because of God's Covenant.

In 1 Samuel we find that man. A man who had the heart of God. The Lord called David, "A man after my own heart," when Samuel was told to go and anoint him king over Israel. Saul had proved that his heart was selfish and disobedient to God and His covenant commands. David, a covenant hearted man, would become the greatest king of Israel and the measuring stick for all kings who would succeed him. To have God's heart he had to be a man of covenant integrity. The Lord is a covenant keeper. David proved that he too was a covenant keeper and a victorious warrior as a result.

When he was just a shepherd boy, before he actually sat on the throne of Israel, David used the covenant to fight his battles. He knew that when you fight with the covenant, God fights with you.
"And Saul said to David, You are not able to go to fight against this Philistine, you are only an adolescent, and he has

been a warrior from his youth. And David said to Saul, your servant kept his father's sheep. And when there came a lion or again a bear and took a lamb out of the flock, I went out after it and smote it and delivered the lamb out of its mouth; and when it arose against me, I caught it by its beard and smote it and killed it. Your servant killed both the lion and the bear; and this uncircumcised Philistine shall be like one of them, for he has defied the armies of the living God! David said, the Lord who delivered me out of the paw of the lion and out of the paw of the bear, He will deliver me out of the hand of this Philistine. And Saul said to David, go, and the Lord be with you." (I Samuel 17:33 - 37)

Saul did not understand the power of covenant living. he was not a man after God own heart. All he could see was the size of the problem, Goliath, and the size of David, a youth. But David did not view things in the same way.

David knew that he had a covenant relationship with the God of the universe. The Creator of all things had entered into covenant relationship with man through Abraham; and he, David, was a son of Abraham. David knew that he carried on his person the scar of circumcision, which identified him with the power and protection of God.

The Lion, the Bear, and the Giant

Notice what he called Goliath. "This uncircumcised Philistine". David made claim to the fact that Goliath was not in the same covenant relationship as he. He equated Goliath the same as the lion and the bear. They too did not have a covenant relationship with the Lord. There would be no difference in the outcome of this fight because of the fact that David was in covenant and Goliath was not.

David also said that it would be the Lord who would deliver him. When you do battle with the covenant on your side, you fight with the power of Almighty God; the Lord becomes your Warrior and your Defence. God is a covenant keeping God; David knew it. The result was victory for Israel and exaltation for David.

David would be the standard for leadership in the nation of Israel. Every king after him would be measured by how David honored God and kept the Covenant of God. There was no other king like him. He was a man after God's own heart.

Right Attitude

David understood personal covenants as well. After the victory over Goliath, David became friends with Saul's son Jonathan. These two became the best of friends, to the point of making a covenant between each other. The covenant of David and Jonathan was a covenant of friendship and protection.

David was being hunted by Saul. Jonathan knew that David would eventually become king. Jonathan promised to keep David informed of the plans of his father, Saul. David promised to protect Jonathan and his descendants[a]. This was not a lightly taken vow. David would keep this covenant regardless of what took place.

When David obtained the throne of Israel and Saul and Jonathan had been killed in battle, the descendants of Saul ran for their lives. They were convinced that David would be ruthless and would murder all the descendants of Saul in order to insure his throne. They did not know the heart of David. They did not know that David had made a covenant with Jonathan to protect his descendants.

Because of the ignorance of covenant, many people believe that God too will be ruthless; and is out to get us. Nothing could be farther from the truth. "God so loved the world that he gave His only begotten son"[b]. Many people run from God because of the lies of Satan, unaware that God is a covenant keeping God. Those who will be in covenant relationship with Him have nothing to fear.

After the death of Jonathan, David is longed to fulfill the covenant vows he had made to him.
"And David said, Is there still anyone left of the house of Saul to whom I may

---

[a]. I Samuel 20:42
[b]. John 3:16

show kindness for Jonathan's sake" (II Samuel 9:1)

David inquired about the descendants of Saul and found that there was one left who was Jonathan's son named Mephibosheth. Mephibosheth was a cripple because of the fear that came on the house of Saul when Saul and Jonathan was killed and David took the throne. His nurse had dropped Mephibosheth when he was five years old while running from David. Now he is a grown man and David inquires about him[a].

David could have forgotten his covenant with Jonathan and just continued as king. The house of Saul had been dethroned and posed no threat to his kingdom at all. But David was a man after God's heart; a covenant man. He had to show kindness. It was in his heart to honor his covenant with Jonathan. It was not just something that he had to do, it was something that he wanted to do. He longed to show kindness to Jonathan and his descendants.

Mephibosheth is brought before David, and all the land of Saul is given back to him; even his servants are restored. But David tells Mephibosheth that he would sit at David's table for the rest of his life. Mephibosheth, who was once an outcast, became the equivalent to the king's son.

This is a beautiful picture of redemption. As

---

[a]. II Samuel 9

sinners, crippled and lied to, we too are called by the King; Almighty God. As we throw ourselves before him in fear of his wrath, he lifts us with forgiveness and mercy and restores us, through His Son Jesus to a seat of honer. We are the Mephibosheths of life, now seated in heavenly places in Christ Jesus[a].

Because of his love, faithfulness and integrity, David became the example for all of the kings to follow[b]. Each king is chronicled by his success or failure to walk in the ways of king David. God's power and provision were released when Israel would return to God and remember His covenant. Judgement would fall on Israel when they would "forget" God.

Throughout the Bible we see the power of this covenant between God and Israel. As long as the nation of Israel would walk in obedience to the covenant commandments, they would be the most blessed people in the earth. Whenever they would stray from the provisions and commandments given by the Lord at Sinai, destruction would result.

Foreign armies could not stand against the Lord and the nation when they were walking in covenant obedience. When an evil king would cause Israel to sin and seek after other gods, they would soon find their nation being conquered or taken into bondage. God is a covenant keeping God, even when Israel was not a covenant keeping nation.

---

[a]. Ephesians 2:6
[b]. I Kings 15:5

The Old Testament is an account of how a nation is protected under this "Blood covenant" with the Lord. It also tells the story of how devastating it is when men break covenant. Blessings come on and over take those who walk in covenant, while curses come on and overtake those who do not[a].

> "But Hazael, King of Syria oppressed Israel all the days of Jehoahaz. And the Lord was gracious unto them, and had compassion on them, and had respect unto them, because of the covenant with Abraham, Isaac, and Jacob, neither cast them from his presence as yet." (II Kings 13:22)

God respected Israel because of Covenant. Even when they were still in sin and disobedience in areas of life. A wicked king named Jeroboam had led Israel into idolatry. But the Lord still heard the prayers of Jehoahaz and brought victory because of the covenant of Abraham, Isaac and Jacob[b].

The blessings and curses of Deuteronomy twenty eight are still evident in the lives of Abraham's descendants. God told Abraham that His covenant would be an "Everlasting Covenant"[c].

---

[a]. Deuteronomy 28
[b]. II Kings 13
[c]. Genesis 17:7

11
THE NEW DEAL

"Behold the days are coming, says the Lord, when I will make a new covenant with the house of Israel and the house of Judah. Not according to the covenant which I made with their fathers when I took them by the hand to bring them out of the land of Egypt, My covenant which they broke, although I was their Husband, says the Lord.

But this is the covenant that I will make with the house of Israel: After those days, says the Lord, I will put My law within them, and on their hearts will I write it; and I will be their God, and they will be My people.

And they will no more teach each man his neighbor and each man his brother, saying, Know the Lord, for they will all know Me [recognize, understand, and be acquainted with me], from the least of them to the greatest, says the Lord, For I will forgive their iniquity, and I will [seriously] remember their sin no more." (Jeremiah 31:31 - 34 Amplified)

The Old Testament is a running account of the power of the covenant. It shows us how God views this covenant relationship as well as how he deals with nations and peoples in response to His covenant. The Prophets of the Old Testament proclaimed the destruction that would come on Israel because of their failure to "remember the Lord' and their rejection of His commandments. Jeremiah, however, makes a dramatic declaration concerning the coming of a new covenant. This covenant was to be distinctly different in nature to the old covenant.

As we have seen in the Old Testament scriptures the covenant that the Lord has honored has always been the same covenant. The law that governed the nation that God called forth through Abraham, was in fact, God's plan to bring a redeemer into the earth. Mysteriously hidden within what has been known as the "law", was the plan of salvation and the legal precedent for the Lamb who would take away the sin of the world.

Even though it has been referred to as the Law, it contained the standards for the direction of the moral, social, and political policy of God's covenant people. A people were to be preserved, through which, the Lord would bring forth the promised seed who would be the "Serpent Crusher". His covenant, though modified by the involvement of Abraham, Isaac, Jacob, and Israel, was still the same promise He made to the woman in the Garden.

Jeremiah's prophetic promise of a new covenant points to the day when the "Serpent Crusher" would be legally able to usher in a "new contract" between God and man. The terms of this new agreement were to be a different relationship than the first covenant.

No longer would it be left in the hands of men to pass down the covenant terms. Under this promised new covenant every man would have the availability of intimacy with the Lord. "For all shall know Me" speaks of the most intimate of relationships. As the Amplified Bible interjects into the verse, this means to recognize, understand and be acquainted with the Lord. The same term is used where "Adam knew Eve and she conceived." The new covenant would have a provision for a personal encounter with the Lord.

No longer would the standards of moral conduct be written on stone tablets. Under the new covenant the standards of government would be placed on the tablets of the heart. Each man would then be responsible for the actions of his own life. The new covenant would have "Heart Circumcision" as part of it[a]. This would mean the "cutting" of the heart, while placing a new righteous standard within men.

No longer would the covenant be mediated by a priest who could only relay the commands and dictates of the Lord through a chain of command. Each man would be responsible for his own relationship to God and for hearing the voice of the Lord personally.

As well as a new covenant relationship, the new covenant had a promise to deal with sin and iniquity. The barrier between God and man was to be abolished once and for all. "I will forgive their

---

[a]. Colossians 2:11

iniquity and I will remember their sin no more." Under the old covenant the sin and iniquities were never forgotten, they were only covered over. Under the atonement, the sins of men were simply covered by the blood of the sacrifices. The word atonement literally means "to cover."

This new covenant was to place iniquity in the realm of forgiveness. The debt that is required because of disobedience was going to be remitted supernaturally. God, the righteous Judge, was going to acquit Israel. He would no longer even remember their sins. Salvation was promised with the new covenant. No longer covered, but redeemed. T h e substitution of an animal's blood, instituted in the atonement, prepared the way for a perfect sacrifice to remove sin once and for all. This promise of a new covenant implies that a better blood would be made available.

12
THE SERPENT CRUSHER

"So the Lord God said to the serpent...I will put enmity between you and the woman and between your seed and hers; he will crush your head and you will strike his heel" Genesis 3:15 NIV

The "Seed' Revealed

The Lord's Covenant was not fulfilled during the time of the Old Testament. No man, king, priest or prophet had totally fulfilled the standard of perfection. The Lord still blessed the nation of Israel whenever they committed to the Law of God. He would overlook their iniquity as long as they presented a suitable substitute in the form of an animal sacrifice. But, still there was no complete fulfillment of the Old Covenant.

The blood of mere animals could not completely remit man's sin. An animal was not qualified to take a person's place; it could only serve as a substitute, until a suitable man could be found. Only a man who had completely fulfilled God's law could act as a mediator in the negotiation of a new law.

Before a new law could be enacted, sin must be dealt with once and for all. Adam's disobedience had lodged sin into every person that came out of Adam's ins. Until that sin was dealt with a New Covenant could not be ratified. God needed a representative from the earth, from the race of man.

Sin had originated in the disobedience of a man, therefore only a man could take the punishment for it. But what man? In order to fulfill the Law of God this man had to be the expressed image of perfection. As the lamb and the bullock that served as a substitute had to be without blemish, so too this man would have to be without blemish. Even Noah, who found grace in the eyes of the Lord and was preserved, did not meet the qualifications of completeness and faultlessness. This new man would have to be unique in all the earth.

Because the covenant was between God and man, God also would have to be present when this new deal was negotiated and ratified. The God of all creation was in covenant with His Man and so He would have to be represented in this New Covenant. Completeness and sinlessness is characteristic of God. He had not broken the covenant. God's representative would have to be the expressed image of God.

Just as in the marriage ceremony, as in all other covenant traditions, this new covenant would involve the presenting of a representative of each family: God and Man. This is the mystery hidden in God and in His statement spoken in the Garden of Eden. The "seed" of the woman would be involved in the crushing of the serpent God was going to arrange for a "serpent crusher" to complete His covenant and to destroy the work of the serpent (Satan).

The Virgin Birth

The prophets of the Old Testament had made various prophetic declarations concerning this coming savior. The most significant to our study is found in Isaiah 7:14.

> "Therefore the Lord himself will give you a sign: the virgin will be with child and will give birth to a son, and will call him Immanuel.(God with us)"

A virgin giving birth is a natural impossibility. The implantation of the spermatozoa into the woman, fertilizing her ovum, thereby causing conception could only be accomplished at the expense of her virginity. That is unless it was done supernaturally by God. But, would that be a man-child or a God-child? By the fact that it was born of a woman it would surely be considered human. But, what about that part that was implanted supernaturally? That part would surely have to be considered divine. The virgin spoken of by Isaiah would then be giving birth to a Man-God, or a God-Man.

You can see why Mary, when the Angel appeared and informed her that she would give birth, asked the question, "How shall this thing be, as I have never been with a man." Gabriel replied that the Holy Ghost would come upon her and the power of the Most high would overshadow her, so that the holy child to be born would be called the Son of God. A God-Man!

This is not simply part of the Christmas story to be passed over as part of religious rhetoric. By causing a virgin to conceive with the implantation of God's power, He would be bringing into existence a new creature. This child would be a unique man who would not inherit the sin nature of Adam. And yet, by all natural means would be born as a human being and would have all the representative characteristics of man. This miracle birth of Jesus is a vital link between the Old Testament and the New Covenant. Jesus was born to be the representative of both families: God and Man. The "seed," promised in Genesis 3:15 was a child named Jesus of Nazareth.

Jeremiah's prophesy of a new covenant meant that a new agreement was to be ratified in the future. In order to create a new "deal," the old contract would have to be fulfilled. God needed a representative that had not broken the old covenant.

With the birth of God's Son, Jesus, the stage was set for the conflict of the ages. The serpent was about to be "taken to task." If Jesus lived up to His potential He would be the absolute champion of the old covenant while ushering in a new covenant that would allow the Lord to forgive our iniquities and remember our sins no more.

In order to be the mediator of a new covenant Jesus would first have to fulfill the old covenant. He would have to be sinless and stay that way throughout His natural life. The old covenant would not be abolished, but rather, fulfilled[a].

The Lord made a promise to Abraham that the covenant would be an everlasting covenant[b]. Today the old covenant is operative in the life of Israel. The Orthodox Jews, while not accepting Jesus as their Messiah, still have the blessings promised to Abraham. The land, the multiplication, and the prosperity of Abraham will still come upon any descendent of Abraham who will claim it in the name of covenant keeping Jehovah God.

Finding a Representative

To complete the preparation for this new covenant between God and man, the mediator would have to be approved by the Lord. As in the marriage covenant ceremony, each representative, bride or groom, would be the ideal of that family. The mediator of this new covenant would have to be the expressed image of the covenant making God. The Covenant representative had to be approved of the Father[c].

Jesus was obligated to walk in the standards of the old covenant. Not until He had accomplished this would He be qualified to be the sacrifice for mankind. In His humanity, Jesus had the potential for success as well as failure. Luke tells us that Jesus grew in

---

[a]. Matthew 5:17
[b]. Genesis 17:7
[c]. Matthew 17:5

stature and favor with God and man[a].

This helps us understand the significance of the fact that Jesus was "in all points tempted like as we are, yet without sin"[b]. Not only can He relate to the daily requirements of life that we experience, He qualified Himself to be the perfect representative from the family of Man.

If The Son Had Failed

Consider the fact that Jesus was tempted, yet without sin - this implies that Jesus could have sinned. The implications of this truth are amazing and wonderful at the same time. What would have happened had Jesus failed in His humanity and succumbed to sin like all the other men and women that preceded and succeeded him?

Consider the fact that Jesus was the incarnate Son of God. In His divinity He was pre-existent. He emptied Himself of all His pre-incarnate glory and made of Himself no reputation, taking on the likeness of man[c]. What would have happened if the "man" Jesus had failed? How would that have affected the "God" part of Jesus?

God cannot lie! Satan is called the "father of lies"[d]. The Word of God declares that those who speak lies have their place in the Lake of Fire. These

---

[a]. Luke 2:40, 52
[b]. Hebrews 4:14b
[c]. Philippians 2:7
[d]. John 8:44

facts are important to consider as we consider the price that was paid and the risk that was taken to get this new covenant in place.

Just suppose that Jesus had failed to live a sinless life. Imagine, if you can, what would have taken place, if on the mountain of temptation, Jesus would have answered Satan challenge with anything other than faith in the Word of God. What if Jesus had responded to the temptation to receive all the kingdoms of the earth, offered by Satan?

If Jesus had not met the requirement of perfection in His humanity, He could not be the "Serpent Crusher". Jesus would have failed to be the "seed of the woman" that God had promised; God would have lied. God would then, by His own word, be a violator of the covenant He made. If Jesus had failed, God would then become servant to the "father of lies." Satan would have won and taken full control of God and all that He created. Satan would be "god of the universe".

Satan is not God, nor can he ever be a god. He does not have the power, as a created being, to rule a universe and maintain a creation. God "upholds all things by the Word of His power."[a] All that exists is "carried" by the power of God in His Word. If God's Word is no good, or if God was a liar, he would no longer have the power to uphold all things. Satan's rule would have been very short lived. As soon as

---

[a]. Hebrews 1:3

Jesus began to bow his knee to Satan, God's Word would have been null and void; and all that is, would have ceased to be. In other words, all that God is, and all that he created would cease to exist because it would no longer have the upholding power of His Word. Everything would cease to be. There would be nothing, surrounded by nothing, in the middle of nothing. Even Satan, (a creation) would have ceased to be, if Jesus had failed.

Praise God Jesus did not fail!

This consideration only begins to shed some light on how much "God so loved the world that he gave His only begotten Son". God took a great risk for you and I. Jesus held in his humanity the potential for failure. But, He being God, also held in his hand the potential for the success of eternity. Jesus became the perfect representative, a lamb without blemish, a man without sin.

Jesus represented both families, man and God. He was born of a woman. He was born from above. He represented the creation as well as the creator. He represented the earth man and the God man. And so, Jesus hung between heaven and earth and shed His blood to ratify the new covenant. He became the sacrifice for both families in covenant.

One Representative, Two Families

On the night that Jesus was betrayed, He shared the passover meal with his disciples. During this meal He begins to look toward the cross when He takes bread and breaks it. This breaking of the bread is not unusual. The Seder meal has three loaves of bread or "Matzo" which until this time represented Abraham, Isaac and Jacob. I believe that Jesus took the loaf that represented Isaac, and by tradition, broke it.

What he did then broke from the tradition of the old covenant passover ceremony. He said, "This is **MY** body which is broken for you". The representation of Isaac was being replaced by the representation of Jesus the Son of God. The bread apparently did not represent Abraham, Isaac, and Jacob; but rather, Father, Son and Holy Ghost.

The Son was being broken in a covenant act. The eating of this bread would be a type of covenant expression from that point on. The sharing of Jesus' body in this covenant act would symbolize the "taking in" of the life of Jesus. Bread being the symbol of the very basis of life, a staple, meant that by eating His body, symbolically, you are taking his life.

"In like manner he took the cup, when he had supped saying, this cup is the New Testament (Covenant) in my blood"[a]. Again Jesus, broke from old covenant tradition by declaring that the new covenant would now be in His blood. Orthodox Jews understood the old covenant to be in the blood of Abraham through the circumcision and through the blood of sacrifices made for atonement. Then Jesus

---

[a]. 1 Corinthians 11:25

told His disciples that this new covenant would have it's ratification in His own blood.

We have missed this significance due to a lack of covenant understanding. We have also missed it through the ignorance of a scientific truth. The blood of the mother is not the blood of the child. Science has found that paternal verification can be done by comparing the blood of the baby to the blood of the father. In other words, the blood type of the child is determined by the blood of the father. Jesus did not have Mary's blood. He had the blood type of the Father. God's blood would be the ratification of this New Covenant!

Meeting the Conditions

In order for a new covenant to be implemented and made active in the earth, all conditions must be met. This would include the completion of God's sacrificial system's requirements.

In order for there to be a sacrifice, the High Priest must be given the lamb so that he can inspect it. Jesus was betrayed into the hands of sinners and presented to the High Priest Caiaphas[a]. This would be the examination of Jesus; The Lamb of God. After finding that Jesus was without blemish, although false charges were brought against Him, the High priest sentenced Jesus to die for the people.
"Now Caiaphas was he, which gave

---

[a]. John 18:13,24

counsel to the Jews that it was expedient that one man should die for the people". (John 18:14)

The High priest of those days offered Jesus on the altar of the cross in compliance with the old covenant. Jesus became the final sacrifice for sin, thereby remitting it[a].

Two Sacrifices

It is interesting to note that two sacrifices were made that day. Jesus was crucified on the Day of Atonement, prior to the Passover Sabbath. At approximately the same hour that Jesus was taken out and nailed to the cross at Calvary, the sacrifice of the Day of Atonement was being placed upon the altar in the Temple court.

It takes time for a person to die the death of the cross. The shedding of blood is not the only cause of this type of a death. Hanging with your arms outstretched causes the need to push up with your feet in order to breath. Death occurs when the legs, because of fatigue and blood loss, can no longer push up. With this strain on the body and the lungs, being completely exhausted, the heart and lungs fail in a very painful expiration. A strong man may last for hours on a cross before death occurs.

It also takes time for a sacrifice to be consumed.

---

[a]. Hebrews 10:12

The burning of the sacrificial animal must result in total consumption. If you have ever cooked a large roast, you know that it takes hours to completely cook that meat. On the altar there is not just a roast, but, the whole animal. It must be reduced to ashes in order for the sacrifice to be complete. It takes approximately the same time to completely burn an animal to ashes as it does to bring death to a healthy man hanging on a cross.

Jesus became the sacrifice for the sins of mankind on the cross. As He died for our sins while the sacrifice of the Old Covenant was also being consumed. The Old and New Covenants were being obeyed by both God and man at the same time. The "Better Sacrifice" was hanging outside the city gates dying for a lost, yet "so loved," world.

The Covenant Lamb.

On the Cross of Calvary the blood of God is shed to ratify the New Covenant. The Levitical Law required the blood of the sacrifice to be taken into the Holy of Holies and offered before the Lord there. As we saw in a previous chapter, Jesus ascended and cleansed the heavenly tabernacle between His meeting with Mary and His meeting with Thomas. Hebrews tells us that he took HIS blood, the blood of the New Covenant sacrifice.

> "In the same way, he (Moses) sprinkled with blood both the tabernacle and everything used in its ceremonies. In fact, the law requires that nearly everything be cleansed with blood, and without the shedding of

blood there is no forgiveness. It was necessary, then, for the copies of the heavenly things to be purified with these sacrifices, but the heavenly things themselves with better sacrifices than these. For Christ did not enter a man-made sanctuary that was only a copy of the true one; he entered heaven itself, now to appear for us in God's presence."

Hebrews 9:21 - 24 NIV

In fulfilling the order of sacrificial offering, Jesus also fulfilled the promise that Abraham made when asked to sacrifice Isaac in Genesis 22:8.

As a covenant partner with the Lord. Abraham was asked to offer Isaac, his son, on an altar of sacrifice. We have heard this story told in many ways. Many times we have heard the explanation of Abraham's faith in God, his faithfulness, his obedience, etc. Abraham knew exactly what he was doing. He was a covenant man. He understood the ramifications of being in a covenant relationship. He was prepared to offer Isaac because he knew that God had to honor His covenant promise to make a mighty nation out of Isaac.

In Genesis twenty two, we read the story of Abraham's "testing". As Abraham and Isaac are going toward the mountain, Isaac asked Abraham, "Where is the sacrifice?". Abraham knew that one of the outstanding characteristics of a covenant is the ability of one covenant partner to ask anything of the other, who can then, in turn require the same. In other words, if God asked Abraham to do something, Abraham could, in turn, require that of

God. This is part of the characteristic of equality. Abraham had given everything to God, for which God was committed to give all He had to Abraham. Jehovah had promised to be a God unto Abraham. Abraham had promised to be a partner in God's covenant.

When Isaac asked that question, "Where is the sacrifice?" Abraham responded with a covenant statement that resulted in the sacrificial death of Jesus Christ. He said, "God will provide Himself a sacrifice!" Abraham was taking His only son to offer him on a hill as a sacrifice. The Lord was obligated to Abraham to take His only Son to a hill and offer Jesus as a sacrifice.

Blessing and Cursing

The Old Covenant was also very explicit concerning what was cursed and what was blessed. Deuteronomy promises blessings and cursing determined by obedience or disobedience respectively. Throughout the Old Testament we see accounts of men and women who received from these promises. Overpowering blessings and disastrous curses are seen throughout the Old Testament narrative. However, the Old Covenant made provision for Jesus to become the sacrifice that would take away the curse.

Jesus becomes cursed by hanging on a tree[a]. Even though sinless, Jesus is made to be sin for us[b]. By becoming cursed according to the Law, He set everybody free from being under the curse of disobedience. Jesus becomes the substitution for those who were violators of

---

[a]. Galatians 3:13
[b]. II Corinthians 3:21

the law. By redeeming us from the curse of the Law, the blessings of the Covenant of Abraham become available through faith in the finished work of the cross.

Executor of a New Estate

Not only did Jesus become our substitute; He became the overseer of the New Testament. Here we begin to see another aspect of this new covenant that Jesus successfully inaugurates with his death.

A covenant is also an expression of the will. A person who enters into covenant does so at his or her own volition. The terms and agreements are in essence their will in written or expressed form.

In our society today we still understand this in terms of a document that a person draws up expressing their desires concerning their estate after they die. A person declares what their will is in a document called a "Will." Another term for this is a "testament." While testament means covenant, it is also defined as a bequest, which means inheritance. Jesus is the surety of the New Testament[a]. He is the guarantee of the Will known as the New Testament.

But no "Last Will and Testament" is of any need or value while the maker is alive. This document called a Will is only empowered by the death of the person who wrote it.

"For where a testament is, there must also of

---

[a]. Hebrews 7:22

necessity be the death of the testator. For a testament is of force after men are dead: otherwise it is of no strength at all while the testator liveth." Hebrews 9:16,17

"...he (Jesus) is the mediator of the new testament, that by means of his death, for the redemption of the transgressions which were under the first testament, they which are called might receive the promise of eternal inheritance." Hebrews 9:15

The death of Jesus ushered in His will as the New Testament or New Covenant. The power of the inheritance is in the death of the one whose will it is. Jesus, The Word, The Son of the Living God, God with Us, has given us His will and activated it by His death. Jesus' death brought the New Testament into effect.

Jesus is not dead though. He is risen. His resurrection allows Him to be the "surety of the New Testament". By dying and being raised from the dead Jesus becomes the executor of His own estate. He has the life, power and authority as the resurrected Lord to administer the New Testament and assure that His will is done. The result is, that as he lives, we are assured that every promise of blessing is "Yes and Amen." We have an eternal inheritance that is administrated by our new High Priest and Apostle, Jesus Christ. We can put our faith in God's Word because we have God's Word, Jesus, on it.

When Jesus was laying down His life, Satan was being defeated and he didn't know it. What looked like death's victory was in fact the total conquering of death,

Satan, and the restoration of all that had been lost in Adam's sin. Amidst all the noise of the crowd, the earthquake and the darkness, Satan couldn't hear it, but Heaven heard the distinct sound of a Serpent being crushed!

Jesus died, was buried, and rose again. He lives for ever to make intercession for us. Jesus is our "Serpent Crusher".

13
A BETTER DEAL

"All power is given unto me in heaven and in earth."
Matthew 28:18

"But now hath He obtained a more excellent ministry, by how much also He is the mediator of a better covenant which was established upon better promises" Hebrews 8:6

In order to fully comprehend the impact of what took place in the spirit realm at calvary and how it relates to our study of covenant, lets recap what we now know.

The covenant of redemption began in the Garden of Eden when The Lord spoke His covenant saying, "The seed of the woman would crush the head of the serpent". That covenant was continued through the salvation of Noah and his family from the waters of the flood.

Abraham was invited to participate in the plan of redemption through the shedding of his blood known as the circumcision. All ancestors of Abraham would be able to participate in Abraham's relationship with God as long as they participated in the shedding of blood; the circumcision of the flesh. Isaac, Jacob and eventually, all of Israel was initiated into this covenant relationship. God honored their obedience as well as their disobedience as seen through the narration of the Old Testament.

In prophetic fulfillment, Jesus is born of a virgin in Bethlehem and a Man-God was prepared to represent both Man and God in negotiating a new covenant.

Jesus has taken Abraham's place in a new covenant relationship. This relationship is different than the relationship that the nation of Israel had. This new covenant called for the forgiveness of sin and the availability of an intimate relationship with God the Father through Jesus Christ.

Jesus is the Lamb of God who took away the sins of the world by offering Himself as a substitute on the altar of the cross. He became the Lamb of God through fulfilling the Old Covenant standards and proceeding through the examination and execution at the hands of the High Priest according to Levitical Law.

Had Jesus simply been crucified at the hands of sinners, the mystery of God would be incomplete. Death was though to be the final say for man. Man could not be free from the result of Adam's sin as long as men died and stayed dead. Jesus was to be the "Serpent Crusher" destroying all the work of the enemy. He had to go beyond death to finalize the "crushing" of Satan.

The Mystery of God

God is a God of law and covenant. He will do nothing except it is connected to divine law and covenant relationship. Even when Adam committed high treason and delivered all his divine authority to the devil, the Lord could not and would not immediately strip him of his authority. God knew a better way. He had a plan. The Apostle Paul called it a "mystery, hid in God from the foundation of the world"[a]

God had to set up a plan to defeat Satan at his own game as it were. Jesus would be the representative and the warrior who would engage this enemy of God on the battlefield of the earth, the cross and hell itself.

As Jesus was hanging on the cross, no doubt the devil could not believe his eyes. Here hung the Son of God, in the hands of sinners, being made a curse as He hung on a tree. He must have thought that a great victory was about to be had and that all of eternity would be his as a result. He did not realize that he was playing right into the hands of the mighty God of all wisdom and power. As I said, "Satan was losing and he didn't know it". Had he known, Paul said, "he would not have crucified the Lord of Glory".

Because our sin was imputed to Jesus and because he was crucified on a tree, Satan must have thought that he had the authority to take him to hell. Hell was not designed for man but for Satan and his angels. Jesus descended into the bowels of the earth

---

[a]. Ephesians 3:9; I Corinthians 2:7,8

and was being held in the "pains of death"[a]

But, here was the deciding violation of Adam's divine authority. Satan took a righteous man into hell. This was beyond the authority that had been given him by Adam. It was perhaps through this "breach of contract" that legal grounds were found for his defeat. Jesus, the second Adam took the keys to death, hell, and the grave, and stripped Satan of all his authority[b].

The resurrection of Jesus from the grave was the final blow in the crushing defeat of the devil at Calvary. Not only had mankind's sin been forgiven, but the "Captain of our Salvation" was alive, proving forever that death had no power anymore. Jesus, the resurrected Lord, made a public spectacle of the devil, triumphed over him in life and in death as well. Praise God Jesus is Lord.

New Mediator

By His position of authority over heaven and earth, He becomes the mediator of a better covenant established on better promises. But how is it a better covenant, and what are the better promises?

Consider first that God the Father is now in covenant with Jesus Christ, the Son of God. Jesus has taken Abraham's place as the Mediator of the New Covenant. No longer is it ratified by the shedding of

---

[a]. Ephesians 4:9; Acts 2:24
[b]. Colossians 2:14,15

the blood of circumcision. It has forever been ratified by the blood of Jesus Christ. It is now not a circumcision made with hands, but our hearts are cut when we come into relationship with Jesus and the Father through Him.

Since Jesus has taken Abraham's place in this New Covenant relationship, our Mediator lives forever. In fact the Mediator of the New Covenant is God; God the Son. The mediators of the Old Covenant were fallible men who at times violated the standards, and their sins had to be atoned for through sacrifices of animals. No mediator or participant in the Old Covenant could claim perfection. All have sinned and come short of the glory of God[a].

Jesus on the other hand did not break the Old Covenant and will not break the New Covenant. God the Father did not break the Old Covenant and will not break the New Covenant either. This New Covenant is, by the relationship of its participants, an unbreakable covenant. That makes it a better covenant.

> "For he has made Him (Jesus) to be sin for us, who knew no sin; that we might be made the righteousness of God in him." II Corinthians 5:21

Because Jesus represents us in this covenant relationship, in Him we become the Righteousness of

---

[a]. Romans 3:23

God. Righteousness is imputed to us through faith in Jesus Christ as if we had never broken His law. Righteousness, literally interpreted is the ability to stand in the presence of God as if sin never existed. Through the substitutionary death of Jesus, and his resurrection, we can enter boldly the Throne of Grace, as if sin was never a problem.

Of course, that does not exempt us from living a holy life, pleasing to the Father. Without holiness no man shall see Him[a]. There remains a responsibility under the spirit of this New Covenant that all partake of his nature and depart from evil.

It is not a legislated holiness walk; but a result of God's love being expressed to us through His Son, Jesus Christ, that we are compelled to walk pleasing to the Lord. A person who is trying to live in sin and claiming to know the Lord is a liar. To know the Lord is to love Him. To love Him is to want to purify yourself from things that are displeasing to Him. We are talking about the character of the New Covenant which we saw in King David, and which we will cover further in upcoming chapters.

Better Promises

Reconciliation to the Father is a better promise of the New Covenant. Being able to stand in His awesome presence and just worship Him is a privilege that was not afforded the participants of the Old

---

[a]. Hebrews 12:14

Covenant. Only the High Priest could enter behind the vail into the presence of the Glory of the Lord. He could only do it once a year on the Day of Atonement.

We have received the "Spirit of Adoption." The Apostle Paul wrote that through this adoption we are reconciled and have the ability to cry "Abba" or "daddy" to our God[a]. The promise made by Jeremiah said that we could all know Him as our sins are remembered no more.

The experience of the New Birth is also one of the better promises. We can be re-born without the plague of sin. To be born from above is a miracle that can only be done by the Holy Spirit through faith, and confession of our faith in Jesus Christ. We can be a new creature in Christ through the experience of the New Birth[b].

What many have yet to see is that when we receive the regeneration of our inner man known as the New Birth, we have a similar "make-up" as Jesus did on the earth. We are not gods neither are we ever going to become gods in the future. However, through the miracle of new birth we have a divine nature born into us at salvation. As Jesus was made up of that which was born of God, we too have that part of us that is "Born from Above".

We still find ourselves faced with temptation,

---

[a]. Romans 8:15; Galatians 4:6
[b]. II Corinthians 5:17

and too many times, let the "carnal" nature win. Jesus was tempted in all points such as we are, but, he showed us how to win every time.

The Word of God was in Jesus. He knew who He was in God. He was the Christ, the Son of the Living God. Do you know who you are in God? You are the redeemed, born from above, more than a conqueror through Him who loved us and gave Himself for us.

We have the indwelling of the Holy Spirit as part of the New Covenant promise. The same person of the Godhead that was the active agent of creation now can live in you through faith in Jesus Christ. You can be "filled with the Holy Spirit". "He is able to do abundantly above all that we ask or think according to the power that worketh within us"[a].

Daniel 11:32 states "They that do know their God shall be strong and do exploits." The better promises are a personal relationship with God the Father, His Son Jesus and the Holy Spirit, through faith.

Not only do we get the better promises, we are also entitled to the blessings of Abraham[b]. Those are the blessings that pertain to wealth and prosperity. God promised to bless Abraham and make him rich. To simply place a money value on wealth is to miss the importance of these very special promises.

---

[a]. Ephesians 3:20
[b]. Galatians 3:13

Wealth is not to be understood as simply financial success and having lots of material possessions. Many misdirected people are trying to use these promises in order to climb the social economic ladder to some sort of success in the natural. Biblical understanding of success and wealth are far different from the world. The world equates wealth with things. God equates true wealth to his plan and purpose.

God promised to make Abraham wealthy. He proved it to the all the nations around him. Israel in obedience to covenant experienced unspeakable wealth. No one has matched the wealth of Solomon yet. Need I say more?

Wealth is more accurately interpreted "financial ability". A person who has unlimited financial ability would be declared by everyone to be a wealthy person. However, no one who merely has money has unlimited financial ability. They are constantly limited by that which is beyond their natural means.

The blessings of Abraham, while promising material goods, has at its root the unlimited availability of God's resources. A believer in Jesus Christ, who is by definition a participant in the New Covenant has as their Father, the God who created the universe; and who, if he needed to, could reward us with tons of gold from a universe of sources. God promised to be a God unto Abraham.

He also promised that in the New Covenant He would be their God too. That, my friend, is financial ability. Whatever God desires to do through His covenant people will not be limited by natural ability. Whether the need is financial, physical, emotional or spiritual, our God is able to make all grace abound to us so that we may always have all sufficiency in all things in order to abound in every good work[a].

No foe could stand against the nation of Israel when they were in obedience to the Covenant of God. Now through Jesus Christ our Lord, we have the ability to stand against every spiritual foe. We have a covenant with God through Jesus Christ. We are in relationship with Almighty God. We are filled with the Holy Ghost, not the spirit of fear. Look out devil you have already lost this Blood War and the Church of Jesus Christ is finding out who they are.

No weapon shall prosper against the Church of Jesus Christ when we walk in obedience and faith. We have God's Word on it and He is a covenant keeping God!

---

[a]. II Corinthians 9:8

14
GET IN AND STAY IN

It was a dark stormy night as the man frantically tried to find a phone booth with a directory. After searching for what seemed like hours he found an empty phone booth. Darting from the car he raced into the torrential rain, aware that his attire this night was not suited for inclement weather. As he reached the phone booth he reached out and quickly grabbed the phone book. "Where was the light?" He strained in the darkness to focus his eyes on the small print while frantically trying to find the elusive number. The rain was pouring in. Everything he had on was becoming more soaked with every oversized raindrop. Suddenly he felt a tug on his jacket. He jerked around to see the rain soaked face of a little boy who said, "Mister, if you get in and shut the door, the light will come on and you'll be out of the rain."

The simple truth of this fictional story is the profound principle of life as it relates to the blood covenant of Jesus Christ. The most important word in the New Testament in regards to covenant is the word "IN". It would be futile to try and list all the times this word is used in the Word.

However, it is the word that describes the position that makes all the difference of eternity. There is no middle ground with this word. You can not be in and still be almost in. You cannot be beside, around, close, next door or above and still be "In". You either are in or you are not in. It is a position from which there is no compromise. You may be "in deep" or "barely in" but you must, in either case, be in or else you are out.

This may sound like a cute meditation on a simple word. You may say its just semantics. But, this word will decide your eternal destiny. You are either in or you are out. To be outside of God's plan is to miss out on all that God has for you. To be in is to enjoy the hope, excitement and all the benefits of knowing that you are saved and that God is on your side.

My father, Charles (Doc) Hix, said to me, "Son, God is not going to get into your boat. Your boat has holes in it. You must get out of your boat and get into His". What he meant was that the key to walking with the Lord was to forsake my disaster prone way of life and to submit to the plan and the purpose of God. I was going to have to get in.

As we have looked at the wonderful plan of salvation and redemption through this study of the Blood Covenant and spiritual warfare we can see that the question is not, can God bless us; but will he bless us. The Word of God answers that question with a resounding yes!

Then why are some Christians experiencing such despair and depravity? Why do the blessings of God and the victory of the cross seem so distant and even missing from some peoples lives? The answer is position. Are you in?

How do we assure ourselves that we are in this

wonderful covenant relationship? What are the conditions and how can I make demands on this fellowship of covenant in Jesus Christ?

As with all covenant negotiations we must first begin with an evaluation of our needs. I believe that too few individuals can stand to bring their hearts to a true self evaluation. We live in the age of the "self made man". The humanistic influence of this age has produced a self-reliance that, while good for personal motivation, makes men think of themselves as self-sufficient. To examine ourselves is to come into a startling realization that we are desperately in need of something or someone.

Even among many successful Christian business men there is this self-sufficiency. If you could get them to answer out of their faith instead of just getting the expected religious answer, many would say that they don't really need God. They have their business, their large salary, their beautiful home and family; what else do they need?. Without realizing it they have forgotten their most prevalent and eternal need; They need the Lord.

When we stop to evaluate ourselves, we see that we can not survive without God. You can try to explain Him away, declare Him dead, or even refuse to acknowledge him. But, the fact remains that everybody has a "God-sized hole in them". People need the Lord.

On a lonely stretch of Interstate highway one night in June of 1980, in the cab of a "big-rig" truck I did a self evaluation. It was then that I realized that without Jesus in my life I had "the Midas touch" in reverse. Everything I did turned to garbage. My life was a mess because I thought I was self-sufficient. I realized that summer night that I needed the Lord more than he needed me.

Like the prodical son I "came to myself". When faced with myself, I was shocked to find that I wasn't as good as I thought. I had missed the point of eternity. I was an outcast. I was in the rain looking for the light. I simply asked the Lord if I could come in.

The first step to getting in, is confessing our need for a Savior. Until we make confession of that one basic truth, we cannot take the next step. In any type of treatment, there must first be an acceptance of the problem that needs a remedy. If an alcoholic won't admit that they have a problem, they can never expect to begin a recovery. We must judge ourselves as sinners needing forgiveness.

Confession and Repentance.

After "coming to ourselves" with the realization of our need for a Savior, we must accept what Jesus has done for us. Jesus has become our Savior through His death and resurrection. We must next make a declaration that Jesus is our Lord and Savior.
> "That if you confess with your mouth
> the Lord Jesus and believe in your heart
> that God has raised Him from the dead,
> you will be saved. For with the heart

one believes unto righteousness, and with the mouth confession is made unto salvation." Romans 10:9,10

Simply confessing Jesus is not enough. You must believe that God raised Him from the dead. You must believe in your heart that Jesus is the resurrected Lord, not just a man who may declare himself a savior; but Jesus, the certified Lord by the fact of His eternal life.

Other figures in history and religion have claimed to be special, and many deceived people have called them "lord." However, they must do their declaring over a tomb which hold the remains of their "Lord". The resurrection of Jesus stands as the unmovable witness that Jesus is indeed Lord over all the earth. Life and death has been conquered by this one man, Jesus Christ, the Son of the Living God. He alone is worthy to be confessed or declared Lord.

Upon this confession of faith, that Jesus is the resurrected Lord, you receive the acceptance of the Father and the forgiveness of sin. The natural response to this wonderful expression of grace should be a determined act called repentance.

The word, repent, literally means to stop moving in one direction, turn and go the other way. When you turn to Jesus, you must naturally turn away from sin. It is no longer your pursuit. Jesus has become your focus in life, and all that you do should be an expression of love to Him for saving you. In other words, don't go back to the life you came out of.

Make a determined change.

> "Do not be conformed to this world but be transformed by the renewing of your mind, that you may prove what is that good and acceptable and perfect will of God". Romans 12:2

The first act of repentance is the submitting of our selfish will. Our examination of ourselves spotlighted those areas where our will got us into trouble. The last act of the selfish will is to give your will to Jesus.

D.L. Moody, the great evangelist of the 1800's was approached by a dance-hall girl. She told him that she really wanted to get saved, but that she just couldn't give up dancing. She loved to dance and she was afraid that by being saved she would not get to do what she wanted, which was dance.

Mr. Moody simply told her not to worry about that. God loves her and knows her heart and that if she would get saved she could do whatever she wanted. So she accepted Jesus as her Lord and Savior and committed her life to him.

A few days later this young girl came back to Mr. Moody and told him that all her desires had changed and she did not want to live the life of a dance-hall girl any longer. She simply turned her will over to Jesus. His life, and love transforms our desires into right desires. We must turn our will over to Jesus.

The next step to making sure that you are all the way "in," is to be reconciled unto the Father. This is not as hard as it may seem. When you accept Jesus Christ as your Lord and Savior, the Father accepts you. When we place our faith in the finished work of the cross we receive forgiveness of sin and are placed within the "household of faith[a]". We must receive that forgiveness in order to accept our place in God's family.

Jesus has paid the price for us to receive full status within the covenant relationship He has with the Father. We become "joint heirs[b]" with Him in His relationship with God. As a joint heir, all that Jesus has is available to us through faith in God and His Son Jesus. We are part of the New Covenant family, adopted in through the work of the cross.

As a covenant partner we must be ready to serve. The attitude of a covenant person is "What can I do for you, my brother!"

> "Let this mind be in you which was also in Christ Jesus, who, being in the form of God, did not consider it robbery to be equal with God, but made of himself of no reputation, taking on the form of a bondservant,...He humbled Himself and became obedient to the point of death, even the death of the cross. Philippians

---

[a]. Galatians 6:10
[b]. Romans 8:17

2:5-8

We must each humble ourselves and make ourselves a servant of God in a covenant relationship.

There are three reasons for entering into a covenant relationship. The very nature of a covenant is found in these three motivations for being in covenant. They are: First, love and devotion; Second, protection and strength; and Third, unity and equality.

God so loved the world that he gave you Jesus. His devotion is beyond comprehension. He loved you even when you hated Him. Regardless of how sinful and anti-God you might have been, Jesus died for you. He loves you and is devoted to you.

God has promised to be our God. Jesus, "our Big Brother" has died and rose again to be the Captain of our Salvation. He has given you His Word, His name, His Holy Spirit, His Authority and all of heaven's angels to help you be the overcomer that you are destined to be.

It is our covenant relationship that gives us protection from the evil one.

> "In righteousness you will be established; you shall be far from oppression, for you shall not fear; and from terror, for it shall not come near you. Indeed they shall surely assemble, but not because of me. Whoever assembles against you shall fall for your

sake... No weapon formed against you shall prosper and every tongue which rises against you in judgement you shall condemn. This is the heritage of the servants of the Lord, and their righteousness is of me says the Lord". Isaiah 54:14-15,17

Finally, you must make the Covenant your authority in life. God's Word is His bond. What He says, He will do. He has promised to save, heal, deliver, prosper, and protect those who are in covenant with Him through Jesus Christ.

I was preaching this truth once when I was confronted by an older preacher. He said" I would never tell you what to preach, but.." I knew when he said "but," I was going to get it. He went on to try to tell me that God has a specific will and a general will. "For instance," he said, "In 1 Peter 2:24 the Bible states 'by His (Jesus') stripes we are healed. It is His general will to heal. Whether or not He will heal you, is his specific will."

I looked at this "man of God" with amazement. "How could a covenant keeping God be double minded when it comes to His Word," I asked. "James 1:17 tells me that every good and perfect gift comes down from the Father of Lights in whom is no variation or shadow of turning." He brushed off my reply, as if I had said "Mary had a little lamb".

Webster's Dictionary describes a mental disorder when a person exhibits "split personalities" as

Schizophrenia. God is not schizophrenic. He is not unstable or double minded. He cannot lie. His Word says exactly what he means. "He is the Lord that heals you[a]."

The Lord of Covenant is not going to say one thing and do another. His Word is His Bond. He has no dual personality that will be generous and then stingy. He will not promise to heal you and then make you sick. The covenant keeping God cannot have two wills. His covenant is His will and He will honor it when we put our faith in Him.

Some have accepted the idea that God is so honest, He can lie and get away with it. They attempt to declare that because God is "sovereign", He can do whatever He wishes, even if it violates His written Word. As we come to better understand the nature and seriousness of covenants, especially one sealed in blood, we can easily see that this kind of thinking is incorrect.

God has bound Himself to His Word. He has sworn His very existence on His Word.
"For when God made a promise to Abraham, because He could sware by no one greater, He swore by Himself." Hebrews 6:13

God is "Sovereign". He has supreme power. He is omnipotent. However, He has sworn that He

---

[a]. Exodus 15:26

would do what He has said in His Word. The promise to Abraham was sworn to by Himself. If God ever failed to honor His promise, He would cease to be God.

"My covenant I will not break, nor alter the word that has gone out of my lips."
Psalms 89:34

We can place our trust in the Lord because He does not change. God is not going to wake up this morning in a bad mood and decide to not do something He has promised to do. If we will stand on the promises of covenant and meet the conditions of obedience, God will come through every time.

Divine Integrity

God has promised to be our God, forgive our sins and allow us to become intimate with Him through the Blood Covenant of Jesus Christ. Jesus offered himself as a sacrifice for us. In doing so He took Abraham's place in a covenant relationship which was sealed in blood. The Blood of Jesus can cleanse us of all sin because it was that blood which was the "Ink" of the New Covenant.

As long as Jesus is Lord, Savior and King, we have an unbreakable covenant through Him. We have access to the Father and are able to make petition for our needs and wants. Jesus is the door to the blessings of Abraham[a] and the blessings of the New Covenant. We have God's Word on it, Jesus. We can put or faith in the integrity of God the Father, Jesus Christ the Son, and the Holy Spirit.

But, can God put His faith in you? Covenants demand integrity. It is the force that all the promises stand on. God's integrity is immutable; it will not change. The Lord is worthy of our faith and trust. He alone is worthy to be obeyed and followed. He will never fail, leave, gossip, betray, slander, or hate you. But, can He say the same about you.

The key to covenant understanding is knowing how to get in and walk in covenant integrity. When He can trust what you are going to do, you have become a person of integrity. Circumstances cannot be allowed to alter our commitments - our word must be our bond.

We enter into the New Covenant the same way Israel entered into the Old Covenant. It must be through faith and obedience. These two elements are the retraining forces of covenant. We must place our faith and submit our obedience. We must make a determination to be people of covenant. Trustworthy and obedient partners in covenant is what the Lord is waiting for.

You must place your faith in the finished work of the cross. The Blood Covenant of Jesus Christ is

---

[a]. Galatians 3:13

the force that saves, heals, delivers, and brings prosperity to the body of Christ. These are only acquired through a determined faith. Faith is not hard to understand when you understand the nature of a covenant.

Faith is a "Yes" or "No" decision. Has God promised? Is God honest? Did Jesus really die for me? And are the promises of the Bible for us today. The answer to all these questions is a resounding "Yes". The Blood Covenant , by nature, requires a decision to be made as to the veracity of God.

Once the decision is made to believe the promises of the Blood Covenant, a decision must be made to adhere to the conditions of the covenant. Obedience is the decision not violate the standards of the New Covenant. Samuel told Saul in 1 Samuel 15:23, "To obey is better than sacrifice". The New Covenant demands the integrity of obedience to Jesus as Lord, and the Holy Spirit as Guide. You must follow the Lord through the leading of the Holy Spirit, and keep your faith placed in the sure promises of God.

When a person decides to be a believer in Jesus Christ and a person of covenant integrity, they become a real problem for the devil. You become dangerous to his plans and devices. A man of covenant faith and obedience has already defeated him. As a new covenant believer, you are destined to experience and maintain the victory that Jesus bought at the Cross. That makes you a major "head-ache" to the works of darkness.

The overcoming force in the earth is not the doubt filled religious systems of today. The overcomers are those who have determined to be men and women of faith. But, faith in what?

> "They over came him by the Blood of the Lamb, and the word of their testimony, and they loved not their lives unto the death." Revelation 12:11

It is our faith in the blood of the New Covenant, the word or integrity of our honest report, and the desire to be all, do all and give all for Jesus Christ, that brings victory. Our adversary, the devil, knows that when we become New Covenant Christians, He cannot keep us sick, poor, discouraged, or hopeless. We know we will win, even against seemingly over powering obstacles, because we are on God's side and He is on ours in covenant relationship.

15
RELATIONAL AUTHORITY

One of the major political concerns of the latter half of the twentieth century has been the proliferation of nuclear arsenals. The availability of nuclear weapons in the world has brought with it the fear that these tremendously destructive devices could fall into the wrong hands. The concern that cruel and barbaric, and even, tyrannical governments could feasibly gain access to nuclear bombs has been a foremost concern within the leading industrial nations. Civilization is immanently threatened by the possibility of a psychologically deranged leader having access to "The Bomb".

While this is a real concern, lets explore the principles behind such a worry. It is not the fact that these awesome forces are available that is at the root of the concern. It is not that these weapons exist that can cause the world to hold it's breath in fright. The root of the concern is a simple principle that also applies to our understanding of covenant.

Awesome power must not be placed into the hands of the irresponsible. A mentally disturbed tyrant with a nuclear bomb sends shutters through us all. The potential for disaster would be tremendous if a Sadaam Hussien was able to use an atomic device whenever he pleased. Poor judgement, irresponsibility and the selfish desires of men like this, could result in mass destruction and the loss of millions of lives. We, as civilized people, are relieved to know that such implements of destruction are out of reach of these "wackos".

The same principle is true in the spirit realm as it is in the natural. Power does not come without responsibility. With power comes authority. Neither power or authority is granted without responsibility. A child cannot be trusted with a 30-30 rifle until they have proved they are able to handle the responsibility.

Another consideration when delegating power is the principle of accuracy. The more powerful the weapon, the more accuracy that is needed. If you miss with a "pea-shooter", little damage is likely to occur. However, if you are aiming and deploying a powerful weapon, such as an atomic bomb, you had better hit where you aim. Innocent lives can be destroyed with the inaccurate use of powerful weapons.

The same is also true in the use of spiritual weapons. Inaccuracy has brought reproach, destruction, and harm to innocent people in the body of Christ. In most cases of personal harm, destruction, and reproach, the cause has not been spiritual warfare, but, the inaccurate use of spiritual weapons; especially that of authority.

The Blood Covenant is our document of authority. Jesus died to bring mankind back into relationship with the Father. That relationship was broke when Adam committed high treason by bowing to the temptation of the devil. The serpent, or the devil, took all of man's authority over God's creation and began to use that authority against God.

The Word of God tells us that Satan offered Jesus all the kingdoms of the world, if He would only bow his knee and worship the devil[a]. Jesus did not dispute the fact that Satan had all these kingdoms. Satan had the authority of Adam and the kingdoms that were previously under Adam's authority.

When Jesus came out of the grave as the resurrected Lord, he told His disciples that "All power had been given unto Him, both in heaven and in earth[b]". This transference of power had been accomplished through His death, burial and resurrection. Jesus "blotted out" the laws and decrees that were against us when he "spoiled principalities and powers" by triumphing over them on the cross[c]. When Jesus ushered in the New Covenant, the authority and power of God and Adam was given to Him as King of Kings and Lord of Lords.

Unity and Authority

> "Verily, Verily, I say unto you, Whatsoever ye shall ask the Father in my name, he will give it you. Hitherto have you asked nothing in my name; ask, and ye shall receive, that your joy may be full." John 16:23,24

---

[a]. Luke 4:5 - 7
[b]. Matthew 28:18
[c]. Colossians 2: 14, 15

Someone once told me that when Jesus, the Truth, says "Verily, verily" or " tell you the truth", I had better pay close attention. Just think, Jesus always spoke the truth. He was truth personified. And yet, He makes an emphatic statement which He precedes with "truly, truly".

The truth of this statement is often missed because of the lack of understanding of covenant. The emphatic statement, "Truly truly", precedes a covenant declaration of authority in the use of the name of Jesus. "Whatsoever you ask the Father in my name" is a declaration of divine authority.

The name of Jesus has been exalted "above every name; that at the name of Jesus every knee shall bow, of things in heaven and things in earth and things under the earth." Every knee includes those of principalities, powers, rulers of the darkness of this world, and spiritual wickedness in high places[a]. All power has indeed been given to Jesus and He has given us use of His name as covenant partners.

The Blood Covenant is based upon the good name of the participants. God and man are in covenant through Jesus Christ. We have the privilege of making covenant request in the name of our representative, Jesus. When Jesus gave us His name, He gave us the power of Almighty God. God has made Himself available to the believer through faith in His Son Jesus. We received the delegation of

---

[a]. Ephesians 6:12

power and authority through the Covenant in Jesus' blood and in the name of Jesus Christ.

Cooperative Fellowship

Let me remind you that a covenant is usually Bilateral. The strength of a covenant is in the mutual participation or fellowship of it's partners. You must enter into covenant relationship in order to receive the blessings of that covenant. You must commit your life to Jesus Christ, placing your faith in Him and the substitutionary sacrifice of the cross. In other words, before you can effectually use the name of Jesus, you must determine to fulfill the conditions of the New Covenant.

Many have failed to realize that the difference between victory and defeat lies with covenant obedience and faith. Many have attempted to bypass the standards of covenant and still receive the blessings that come from being in covenant. The idea that you can get all you want without conditions is simply irresponsible. It is this failure in many Christians that has led to serious consequences, many of which have been blamed on God.

If a woman were to arbitrarily declare herself to be the wife of this author, she would not yet be able to benefit from that marriage. In fact, if she did not enter into a marriage covenant, legally and scripturally, with me; she could be said to be "taking my name in vain." Only one person, Renee Harrison Hix, has the covenant right to call herself, Mrs. Randy Hix. Because of our covenant relationship she alone has the authority of wife, mother and partner in ministry to me. But, that authority does not come without the responsibilities of our marriage.

Failure to live to the standards of covenant has caused many to live below the privileges of the New Covenant. Many have entered into this New Covenant, only to immediately break the standards through willful disobedience. If you are going to name the name of Jesus, be in covenant with Him. To not serve Jesus in this New Covenant, and yet call yourself a Christian is like "taking the Lords name in vain".

But what are the stipulations of the New Covenant? How should I live after I have made Jesus Lord? The criteria for obedience has not changed.

> "And it shall come to pass, if thou shalt harken diligently unto the voice of the Lord thy God, to observe and to do all his commandments which I command thee this day, that the Lord thy God will set thee on high above all the nations of the earth, and these blessings will come on you and overtake thee." Deuteronomy 28:1

The character of the Old Covenant and the New Covenant has changed. The old Covenant was the letter of the Law, while the New Covenant is the Spirit of the Law. "The Letter kills, but the Spirit gives life.ᵃ" The Old Covenant is fulfilled in the New Covenant through the spirit of faith and obedience.

Hearken to the Voice of the Lord.

We must understand how the Lord speaks today. He has given us His Word. It is the written Word of God that has been given as a love letter to the Church of Jesus Christ, his bride. It is through the written Word that we hear the instructions of right living and moral conduct. It is our "Sure Word of Prophesy"ᵇ. It is a divine guide to live by. Every question that deals with life has an answer within the pages of the written word.

The Word of God is the Covenant of God. It contains the promises of God and the conditions that must be met before God can release his blessings. Too many have failed to understand that the answers to life's problems have already been spoken in God's Word.

The Lord also speaks through anointed ministers who have been given to us by Jesus Himselfᶜ. These ministers are sent to equip us for the work of the ministry. These voices of the Lord are not to be ignored. Covenant blessings can come upon a believer who will listen to Godly counsel. Many have stormed into defeat by not harkening to these voices of the Lord.

ᵃ2 Corinthians 3:6
ᵇ. 2 Peter 1:19
ᶜ. Ephesians 4:11

The voice of the Lord also comes to our regenerated human spirit by the Holy Spirit within us. The "still small voice' of the human conscience is a strong guide when God wants to speak. By reading His Word, listening to those Jesus has placed in our lives and listening to the "witness of the spirit" we have no problem meeting this first prerequisite for covenant blessings.

Follow His Commandments

Jesus summed up the Law by fulfilling the spirit of it. He declared that if a man would do two things he would fulfill the Law of God. First you are to love the Lord with all your heart, soul and strength. It is not hard to love someone so lovable. The more you know Him the more you love Him. To love the Lord with everything you have is the first commandment of the Old Covenant and the first commandment of the New Covenant. It is this love that makes you want to serve Him and be all that you can be for Him.

The second is not as easy. It is to love your neighbor as yourself. That includes those who are unlikable. Love is a choice that must be made by the covenant believer. It is a condition to covenant blessings. It can be done. God's love has been given to us so that we can accomplish this command. The love of God never fails. You will find that this decision to love is the hardest, but the most rewarding.

Do His Word

Many Christians have failed to achieve victory in their Christian lives because they will not do the Word. They have been programmed by a secular society to respond "normally". They have accepted the mediocre standard that the world has said is the "status quo" as their measuring stick. God has much more blessings for the believer to walk in than you could ever imagine. They are not hard to find. They are written in His Word. A failure to do the Word is what James called "deceiving yourself[a]".

Jesus declared that those that hear His Word and do it is like a man who builds his house on a rock[b]. The storms of life are going to beat on your house regardless of where you build it. In the declaration of Jesus He said that the storm hit both houses. The man who built his house on the rock had victory over the storm. The devil would love to "huff and puff and blow your house down." He can not succeed when you build your house upon the rock of "acted on Word." Do the Word and do not be a forgetful hearer.

The New Covenant Christian must act like a believer. The tell-tale signs of a believer are found in Mark 16:15. When faith begins to take hold on your heart you will begin to see why "these signs follow them that believe". An active faith in the Covenant of Jesus produces results. The power of God is available to the believer through faith in Jesus Christ. This

---

[a] James 1:22
[b] Matthew 7:24-27

power and authority does not come without covenant responsibilities.

16
BE A WINNER

Our commission is to "show forth the praises of him who has called us out of darkness"[a]. The calling of every believer is to be a praise unto His Glory. All that we do and say should bring glory to God. He is the One who we adore, and lift up before men. Our covenant brother has won the victory.

The enemy of God, Satan, has been successful at robbing God of the Glory that He so richly deserves. He has weakened the Church through covenant ignorance. He has attempted to steal the truth of covenant from the Body of Christ with theologies that in essence give credit to the Devil and all the blame to God for defeat. The Church has failed to display the power of God to the degree that it could because men have been ignorant of their covenant privileges. But, no more!

The Lord is raising up a new breed of Christians who will stand firm against the devil and his attempts to defeat, weaken, and deceive. God's people, called by His name, need not be destroyed for the lack of knowledge. The Lord has placed into our hands the tools and weapons necessary to win every battle we face. The most effective weapon in the hands of the New Testament warrior is our relationship with the Almighty God through the blood of Jesus Christ.

Position Yourself

---

[a]. 1 Peter 2:9

The covenant relationship which Abraham had with God produced a righteousness, or "right-standing" with God that allowed him to dictate the articles of destruction or salvation of a city. God has placed within covenant relationship the ability of a men, in righteousness, to "stand in the gap" for their cities, state or nation. Our God has never failed to fight for and defend those who were in right standing with Him in covenant.

It is time for us, as believers in Jesus, and through our relationship in Him, to begin to take back what the devil has tried to steal. We have the relational authority to stand as a spiritual mediator for our homes, our cities, and our nation. Our authority, our inheritance, our Holy Spirit imparted gifts, and callings, demand that we position ourselves to be a winner in Jesus Name.

It is through the Blood of Jesus that we position ourselves for victory and success. The weapons of our warfare are mighty and powerful covenant weapons. The Apostle Paul said "take the Sword of the Spirit, which is the Word of God"[a] to fight against the principalities, powers, rulers of darkness of this world and spiritual wickedness. The Sword is the Covenant of Jesus Christ. It is the Blood Covenant in His blood. The church must rise up in this day with the Covenant of Blood as a powerful weapon in their hand.

---

[a]. Ephesians 6:17

Fear Not!
Do not be afraid to fight with the Covenant of Blood. It is through the blood of the Lamb that we overcome the evil one. Our covenant Brother has joined us in the battle and has already won the victory at Calvary. With Covenant Blood we fight the fight of faith. The blood of Jesus is the mark of the New Covenant Family of God[a].

That "uncircumcised" enemy, the Devil, has been defeated by the Lion of the Tribe of Judah. We now have a circumcision of the heart to show that we are in covenant with our heavenly Father through Jesus Christ. We have become "Blood-heirs" of the promise[b].

FINAL NOTE

This cannot be considered an exhaustive study of the truth of Blood covenant or Spiritual Warfare. It can only be a starting place for your personal study. I pray you can now see that without an accurate understanding of the Blood Covenant and our position of authority in Spiritual Warfare, much of the truth of the Word of God can remain a mystery. As you begin your journey into covenant understanding, I know it will become as strong a force in you as it is intended to be in all of us.

---

[a]. Galatians 4:5
[b]. Galatians 3:14

About the Author

Randy Hix has spent his life involved in Church. In the early 1950's, his parents helped build a strong Pentecostal Church in Newhall, California where Randy was born and raised. Having grown up during the era of the great tent meetings and the growth of the pentecostal charismatic movements, Randy is qualified to speak to the victories and short-comings of that day and bring clarity and accuracy to the body of Christ concerning the move of God today.

Although he was called to preach when he was a teenager, he became involved in music, becoming a semi-professional singer. After years of rebellion, Randy recommitted his life to Jesus Christ and entered the ministry in 1980. He has since become recognized as a solid pastor, leader, and dynamic teacher of Bible truth. Randy Hix is known for his expository teaching and preaching, with revelation, on vital subjects from the Word of God.

Randy and Renee Hix make their home in Southern California, as they serve as Dean at Spirit Life Bible College in Costa Mesa, California; a ministry of Embassy Christian Center and Roberts Liardon Ministries. He is also Director of Life Ministerial Association and Legacy Ministries International, Inc.

The Teaching Ministry of Randy Hix

A Better Covenant Workbook & 12 tapes $50.00
(LM050) A complete audio study of the truth of the Blood Covenant.

**Sex, Love & Other Misunderstandings
About the family . . . . . . 6 tapes $30.00**
(LM052) What does the Bible say about love, marriage and child raising. How to build a strong family.

What is Balance . . . . 4 tapes $20.00
(LM054) What is this thing called "balance" and do you have it?

Dangerous Christianity . . . . 6 tapes $30.00
(LM056) How to be a threat to the kingdom of darkness.

God's Powerful Army . . . . 6 tapes $30.00
(LM058) Will you accept your enlistment call?

Heroes of Faith . . . . 6 tapes $30.00
(LM060) What did Noah, Moses, Abraham and Melchezedek do and how can we become a hero for God?

Answering the High Call . . . . . . 4 tapes $20.00
(LM062) God has called you to a high call. Will you answer yes?

Kingdom Principles . . . . 6 tapes $30.00
(LM064) How to live in the blessings of God's kingdom.

Characteristics of A Warrior . . . . 6 tapes $30.00
(LM066) Are you a warrior? What does one look like?

Holiness . . . . 4 tapes $20.00
(LM068) What is holiness and how do I get it?

Your Call to Intimacy . . . . 2 tapes $10.00
(LM070) The principles of worship and a life of praise.

To order

Products are no longer available

New Address:
P.O. Box 17098 Reno, NV 89511

Or use o1

Order Form
Legacy Ministries

Quantity	Item #	Description	Price	Total
		Sub-total	-------	$
		Shipping cost	-------	$
		Total Amt Enclosed	-------	$

In the U.S. add for shipping:
   1 - 4 items = $ 4.00
   5 - up   "   = $ 6.00

Outside U.S. add for shipping:
   1 - 4 items = $10.00
   5 - up   "   = $15.00

Mail with check or money order to:
Legacy Ministries International
P.O. Box 5370-565
Santa Ana, CA 92704